Women
on Probation
and Parole

THE NORTHEASTERN SERIES
ON GENDER, CRIME, AND LAW
Editor: Claire Renzetti

For a complete list of books available in this series,
please visit www.upne.com

MERRY MORASH

Women on Probation and Parole

A FEMINIST CRITIQUE OF COMMUNITY PROGRAMS & SERVICES

NORTHEASTERN
UNIVERSITY PRESS
Boston

Published by
UNIVERSITY PRESS OF
NEW ENGLAND
Hanover and London

NORTHEASTERN UNIVERSITY PRESS

Published by University Press of New England

One Court Street, Lebanon NH 03766

www.upne.com

© 2010 Northeastern University Press

All rights reserved

Manufactured in the United States of America

Typeset in Arnhem Blond and The Serif Semi Bold

by Integrated Publishing Solutions

University Press of New England is a member of the
Green Press Initiative. The paper used in this book meets
their minimum requirement for recycled paper.

For permission to reproduce any of the material in this
book, contact Permissions, University Press of New England,
One Court Street, Lebanon NH 03766; or visit www.upne.com

Library of Congress Cataloging-in-Publication Data

Morash, Merry, 1946–

Women on probation and parole: a feminist critique

of community programs and services / Merry Morash

Northeastern University Press.

p. cm. — (The Northeastern series on gender, crime, and law)

Includes bibliographical references and index.

ISBN 978-1-55553-723-4 (cloth: alk paper) —

ISBN 978-1-55553-720-3 (pbk.: alk. paper)

1. Female offenders. 2. Crime—Sex differences. 3. Women drug

addicts—Rehabilitation. I. Title

HV6046.M627   2010

364.6'20820973—dc22   2009046308

5 4 3 2 1

CONTENTS

Many of the data that are the basis for this book were collected with resources from Grant No. 96-IJ-CX-002, from the National Institute of Justice. That support is much appreciated, though the analysis and conclusions do not represent the opinions of the National Institute of Justice or its employees. Dr. Timothy S. Bynum, Michigan State University, acted as the coprincipal investigator for that research, and he brought tremendous experience, skill, and energy to the extensive data collection phase of the study. Graduate students who have now gone on to be professors at various institutions were instrumental in that phase of the research. They include Barbara Koons-Witt, University of South Carolina; Kristy Holtfreter, Arizona State University; and Hoan Bui, University of Tennessee. Numerous interviewers assisted with the time-consuming data collection. Probation and parole officers as well as program staff at both of the study sites were patient and helpful throughout that long process. Suyeon Park and Tia Stevens, current Ph.D. students, played a major role in developing the case database for the qualitative data analysis and spent long hours doing tedious work to pull data from multiple sources and assemble the information for qualitative analysis. I owe much to Dr. Eileen M. Roraback, Associate Director of the Michigan State University Public Humanities Collaborative, who applied her talent for writing, supportive friendship, and good advice to the completion of this book. Dr. Nicole Rafter and Dr. Barbara Owen provided substantial advice on the publication process. Much thanks also to Phyllis Deutsch from the University Press of New England, and to Claire M. Renzetti and Christine E. Rasche, who reviewed early versions of the book. The University Press of New England administrative, marketing, and copyediting staff also contributed substantially to preparing the final version of the book and making it available to interested readers. Last but never least of the people who provided support as I carried out the research, analysis, and writing are my husband, Edward Morash, and our children, Valerie and SooJin. They provided exceptional encouragement and a happy home life that freed me to spend time on this project.

Introduction
Research Purpose and Design

I first saw gender-responsive probation and parole services in action while on research site visits to two programs, one on the West Coast and one in the Midwest. At both sites, the female supervising officers were excited about working with women offenders. They differed from the many officers I have met over the years who prefer to work with male offenders because, in the officers' words, women are "manipulative," "too hard to supervise," and "cry and whine too much." During the site visits, the officers expressed pride in their expertise in managing all-woman caseloads. They relished the challenge of meeting the multiple needs of women who struggled with addiction, parenting, child custody problems, violent partners, and inadequate income.

At one of the sites, the officers had set up office space in a neighborhood accessible by public transportation. A mix of office furniture, chairs and sofas in living-room style, and children's play areas gave the space a homey, comfortable feel. Assorted toys and equipment for children, clothing for women, and other potentially useful secondhand items filled one of the rooms. The officers drew on personal networks and charity organizations to stock the room with items that poor women might need, especially when just released from prison or jail.

One supervising officer I interviewed alternated between two cellphones, so one was always charged. She answered a call from one of the women she supervised. The woman's teenage son had some problems at school and "took off." In response to the call, the officer and I dashed out to her car. We spent an hour cruising up and down local streets searching for the young man, the officer all the while updating his worried mother by phone. The officer spotted the young man, called him over to the car, chatted with him briefly, and drove him home. Her phone rang again, and she switched her attention to helping yet another woman in crisis.

Like the probation and parole officers I met on site visits, researchers and theorists have been enthusiastic proponents of gender-responsive corrections, which would provide programming to respond to women's unique needs. I heard their talks at federally sponsored workshops and national conferences, and read their papers. However, the scholarly community was not of one mind. An emerging literature from feminist researchers (Erez 1989; Hannah-Moffat 1999; Shaw 1996), who are attuned to the complex ways in which gender oppression is perpetuated, criticized gender-responsive corrections for two unintended, negative consequences: first, some gender-responsive programs increase control and punishment; and second, some gender-responsive programs fail to open opportunities for women and actually reinforce narrow gender stereotypes, limiting women's role to parenting and traditional occupations, such as beautician or cook. The discrepancy between proponents and critics piqued my interest in how real-world gender responsive programming impacted women.

I was fortunate to receive a National Institute of Justice research grant that allowed me to gather detailed information on women offenders at one of the sites, as well as in a nearby county using traditional supervision. Initially, I envisioned a quantitative analysis to compare outcomes across counties. As I sorted through the women's interviews, supervising officers' case notes and survey responses, and official records of arrests, I realized that the way I had planned to do the analysis would not show the complex differences between the counties. Women's uneven progress in stopping drug use and criminal behavior could not be captured by a simple comparison. As a result, I reorganized the data into qualitative case studies and used an inductive approach to understanding women offenders and the nature and effects of gender-responsive supervision. The research process provided new insight into the little-known world of probation and parole officers, whose work with large numbers of women on a day-to-day basis has tremendous impact on both individuals and society at large.

No previous research on community supervision for women approaches the scale and depth of the study presented in this book. This book provides a close, critical examination of the nuances of the lives of women on probation and parole in two adjacent counties that use very different approaches to supervision. The county I call "Gender Responsive County" is part of a national movement to improve the corrections system by addressing a wide range of needs unique or common to women offenders. In the same state, "Traditional County" employs a much more widespread approach that treats women no differently than men. Traditional County supervision emphasizes monitoring people on probation and parole to ensure that they meet conditions set by the court to avoid incarceration.

This study shows how gender-responsive supervision promotes positive changes in women's lives. By contrast, traditional supervision more often leaves women with limited oversight, little access to resources, and weak or nonexistent relationships with supervising officers and staff in employment, substance abuse, and other critical service programs.

INCREASING NUMBERS OF WOMEN
ON PROBATION AND PAROLE

The large and growing number of women on probation and parole makes this research especially important. U.S. courts sentence a staggering number of women to community supervision — either probation instead of incarceration, or parole from prison at the end of a sentence. In 1995, probation and parole officers supervised almost three-quarters of a million women (Glaze and Bonczar 2007). By 2006, the number had risen to over a million (1,016,886) on probation alone, with another 95,784 on parole: a total of 1,112,670. In just one decade, there was a 56 percent increase in women on probation or parole, amounting to nearly another 400,000 women. Additionally, from 1995 to 2006, the proportion of women in the total population on probation grew from 21 percent to 24 percent, and in the total population on parole from 10 percent to 12 percent. In terms of the growth rate in parole and probation, women outpaced men.

Similar dramatic increases in the number of women in prison drove up the numbers who were released on parole. By mid-2006, three decades of the so-called war on drugs and "get tough" sentencing had resulted in almost three-quarters of a million women serving time in U.S. prisons and jails (Mauer and Chesney-Lind 2002; Richie 1996; Sabol, Couture, and Harrison 2007, 5; Wellisch, Prendergast, and Anglin 1994). Many prisoners released on parole are reincarcerated for violating supervision requirements. In an unfortunate cycle, the growth in incarceration increases the number of women on parole, while failures on probation and parole contribute to the growth in incarceration.

Incarceration drains state and federal resources and disrupts communities and families. For example, some states cannot increase funding for schools because of incarceration costs. Offenders also experience the negative effects of incarceration. Specifically, the close quarters within prisons and jails promote ties among lawbreakers. Prison breaks up families and cuts offenders' ties to community resources. To avoid the cost and other negative effects of incarceration, federal and state policymakers increasingly promote community supervision to keep offenders out of prisons and to assist them after incarceration (Clear 2007; Research Triangle International and Urban Institute 2004). These trends provide additional reason for examining alternative approaches to community supervision for women.

THE PROMISE OF GENDER-RESPONSIVE CORRECTIONS

Considerable research supports the belief of proponents of gender-responsive corrections that women offenders need and benefit from an extensive array of gender-relevant services (Belknap 1996; Bloom et al. 2003; Covington 1999; O'Brien 2006; Owen and Bloom 1995; Richie 2001). Women in prisons and jails throughout the United States have limited education and work experience (Ditton 1999). Up to one-quarter of women prisoners report a past overnight stay in a mental hospital or mental illness (Ditton 1999; also see Steadman et al. 2009). The actual proportion is probably higher, since people commonly conceal mental health problems and treatment to avoid stigma. Incarcerated women report high rates of physical, sexual, and emotional abuse as children, and intimate partner violence and sexual assault as adults. They are often physically unhealthy, especially when they have a history of drug use. Some women use drugs to dampen strong negative feelings rooted in backgrounds of abuse and hardship (Bush-Baskette 2000; Johnson 2004, 12; Kearney 1998, 500; Young, Boyd, and Hubbell 2000). In addition to problems with drugs, alcohol, and mental illness, women in the justice system face parenting challenges posed by troubled children, and difficulty keeping and regaining custody of their children (Bates 2001; Bloom and Steinhart 1993; Boyd 1999; Gabel and Johnston 1995; Seymour 1998).

Surviving in the community is difficult for women on probation and parole (Schram et al. 2006). They struggle to meet their own and family members' basic needs; to access substance abuse treatment; and to obtain social welfare, employment, education, mental health services, and housing (Allard 2002; Austin, Bloom, and Donahue 1992; Koons et al. 1997; O'Brien 2001; Parsons, Warner-Robbins, and Parsons 2002; Richie 2001; Rumgay 2004). One woman parolee in Illinois communicated the importance of meeting multiple needs when she compared avoiding reincarceration with baking a cake (O'Brien 2001). She explained that success required all the ingredients — any single unmet need could make it impossible to survive in the community and avoid crime.

Growing evidence of women offenders' needs has accelerated the push to develop relevant programming. *Wraparound services* and *continuum of care* are terms for an array of relevant services. Ideally, coordinated wraparound services are delivered through multiple providers that address women's varied goals and needs (Bloom, Owen, and Covington 2004; Covington and Bloom 2003; Reed and Leavitt 1998). The term *continuum of care* connotes adapting goals and services over time. Effective programs for women offenders must simultaneously and successively address multiple problems, including poor self-esteem, history of trauma and abuse, pregnancy, parenting, physical and mental illness, substance abuse, and offender-specific barriers to obtaining help.

GENDER STEREOTYPING IN GENDER-RESPONSIVE PROGRAMS

As previously noted, a strain of feminist research raises concerns about whether, in the real world, gender-responsive strategies effectively challenge gender stereotyping and oppression. A study of official records of 500 people on probation in Ohio in the 1980s suggests that this is a valid concern. The study found that probation met women offenders' needs in a way that reinforced two incorrect assumptions (Erez 1989): first, women's roles are limited to parenting; and second, most of the women who break the law are caused to do so by their intimate partners. As a result, women's probation emphasized parenting and intimate partner relationships. In contrast, programming for male offenders concentrated on their need to get good jobs and remain employed. The Ohio study suggests that, unless precautions are taken, correctional supervisors will not objectively assess problems, but will instead depend on misleading stereotypes about the roles and motivations of women offenders.

At least three studies provide more recent evidence that in some settings, a needs-based approach for women offenders reinforces gender stereotypes. To achieve the ideal of gender-responsive programming, Maryland established four jail-based, therapeutic community programs. Women's sessions concentrated on spirituality and aftercare—counseling and group sessions following release—and neglected significant needs like psychological treatment and vocational training (Buffard and Taxman 2000). More-structured parallel programs for men concentrated on building their motivation and preventing relapse. Another recent study in Cook County, Illinois, shows that probation rarely addresses women's high need for substance treatment and job-related services (Mullany 2002). Finally, a multinational study surveyed staff at many institutional and community correctional programs (Bertrand 1999). The program developers explicitly designed interventions to avoid old stereotypes of women in parenting and household maintenance roles. Contrary to their intent, the programs inadvertently reproduced these stereotypes. Signaling that parenting was more valued than other roles, mothers whose children lived in the correctional facilities were given better living quarters. The programs also emphasized home beautification trades (e.g., flower arrangement) over better paid occupations. Stereotyping led to training women offenders for low-paying work rather than more lucrative trades like construction (Lahm 2000). What is particularly disturbing is that programs intentionally designed to embody the ideals of gender-responsive programming in fact did the opposite. Limiting and damaging gender stereotypes were reinforced in the name of gender-responsive programming.

CONCERNS ABOUT EXCESSIVE CONTROL IN GENDER-RESPONSIVE PROGRAMS

The second concern that feminist scholars raise is that gender-responsive programming promotes excessive control of women in the justice system. Needs-based community supervision that promotes what is called intensive supervision can lead to this result. Some probation and parole departments continue to use intensive supervision programs, first instituted in the 1980s (Clear and Hardyman 1990). Designed to protect the public and reduce crime, this approach expanded offender behavior requirements and increased surveillance, detection, and punishment for violations (Fulton, Gendreau, and Paparozzi 1995; Petersilia and Turner 1993). Intensive supervision practices encompass some aspects of the Gender Responsive County style of supervision: frequent drug testing, careful monitoring of behavior, and increased contact with supervising officers. Research on intensive supervision demonstrates that heavy monitoring increases returns to jail and prison for violating the conditions of supervision, but does not reduce serious crimes (Petersilia and Turner 1993). This contradicts explicit gender-responsive correctional goals of keeping women law abiding and in the community by meeting their needs. Intensive supervision tactics may inadvertently contribute to the failure of gender-responsive supervision.

Intensive supervision programs are varied, and some produce better outcomes than others. Most programs stress monitoring and sanctions to the exclusion of referrals and treatment; more-successful programs balance monitoring and sanctions with social casework and substance abuse treatment (Gendreau, Goggin, and Fulton 2001; Paparozzi and Gendreau 2005). Throughout this book, I question the styles of supervision in the two counties, and their impact on the balance between treatment and punishment. Ultimately, the question is whether gender-responsive supervision puts women in prisons and jails, or helps keep them in the community.

Gender-responsive program staff may also increase controls over offenders if they assume the severity of needs indicates a risk of either violence or recidivism. Assuming needs and risks are equivalent justifies increased control and punishment for the neediest women (Hannah-Moffat 1999). Feminist reforms in Canada did lead to gender-responsive prison programming with increased control and punishment (Shaw 1996). The prison required the most treatment and security for women with histories of self-injury, abuse, or mental illness. Program staff had women attend programs to address needs (assumed to be risks) stemming from their backgrounds and circumstances (Hannah-Moffat 1999). The Intensive Healing Program, a closed unit for violent and high-needs women, epitomized the transformation of needs into risks. It placed women with low risks but high needs in restrictive settings designed to control violent women. Because poverty creates many of the very needs that some correctional programs view as risks, the excessive control had the greatest impact on the poorest women of racial and ethnic minority groups (Monture-Angus 2000, 57). Given findings that needs may be recast as risks, I examined the data for evidence that this happened in Gender Responsive County, with its gender-responsive approach.

RESEARCH QUESTIONS AND SETTING

I believe in the strong potential for positive outcomes from gender-responsive probation and parole programs for women. However, other feminist theorists challenge this belief, citing evidence that, in practice, gender-responsive programs produce negative, unintended effects. Conflicting assessments of gender-responsive programming are addressed in the study, with empirical research that answers the following questions:

(1) How does community supervision differ in form and outcome in Gender Responsive and Traditional Counties?

(2) Does community supervision in either county reinforce gender stereotypes for women — for example, by emphasizing parenting to the exclusion of preparation for employment?

(3) Does gender-responsive supervision result in the unintended consequence of increased control and punishment, including incarceration?

I probe these questions deeply, using multiple sources of data on women during their twelve months of community supervision. The analysis is structured to seek answers to questions for several subgroups of women, differentiated by crime patterns and life circumstances. To set the stage for this exploration, I next describe the methodology and the research setting, including the differences between Gender Responsive and Traditional Counties.

The project's research staff collected data between 1997 and 1999 in two adjacent counties within the same northwestern U.S. state. A statewide system of community supervision imposes key similarities in probation and parole services across all counties. County-based offices of the Community Supervision Agency handle probation cases referred by the courts, and parole cases for people released from jail or prison. Since the same staff handle probation and parole caseloads, I refer to them as supervising officers. These officers are expected to ensure that probationers and parol-ees comply with conditions set by the judge or the parole board. Typical conditions are avoiding drug and alcohol use, paying restitution, obtain-ing gainful employment, not associating with people who have broken the law, completing community service, and attending self-help and treat-ment programs. Alcoholics Anonymous and Narcotics Anonymous groups are the most frequently required self-help programs. Mandated treatment focuses on substance abuse or mental illness.

Community supervision officers apply a statewide point system to es-tablish recidivism risk and danger to the community. High-risk scores re-flect such things as prior drug-related convictions, violence, and previous incarcerations. Point ranges correspond to recommended intensity of su-pervision. Supervising officers can impose a supervision level that corre-sponds to the risk score. In addition, they can increase the risk score, in which case they must provide a rationale in the official records. After first meeting with a woman, officers can also decrease the level of supervision. Again, they must note the reasons in the official records. The higher the level of supervision, the more required office visits, urine analysis tests to detect drug use, and supervising officer visits to places of residence and employment.

Throughout the state, the limited level of supervision requires women to pay a supervision fee and any court fines, restitution, or other costs; to not leave the state without permission; to work or attend school unless there is a valid reason not to; and to avoid breaking the law. Limited super-vision does not require women to report to or talk with the supervising officer. Low, medium, and high levels of supervision stipulate different degrees and combinations of reporting by mail and personal or phone con-tact. Officers can require mental health and substance abuse evaluations, drug tests, counseling, and treatment. Offenders are responsible for the cost of drug testing, mental health or substance abuse evaluations, and treatment. Thus, for many women, community supervision requires that they apply for and use medical insurance.

The supervising officer notes any violation of probation or parole condi-tions in the official record. Supervising officers sanction women for viola-tions or refer them back to court, where a judge may sanction them or re-voke their community supervision. Women who lose contact with their supervising officers are officially in a status called *absconded*, which is a violation of supervision requirements. Absconded status often results in revocation, which means that women are put in jail or prison. Alternatives to incarceration, called sanctions, include punishments ranging from a day to months in jail or the work release center, or hours of community service work, such as picking up highway litter. Supervising officers also use treatment-oriented sanctions, like increased drug-testing, greater contact with supervising officers, and participation in outpatient or residential treatment programs.

Supervising officers and judges divide responsibilities somewhat differently in the two counties. When women violate conditions of supervision, Gender Responsive County officers usually ask them to agree to a sanction instead of returning to court. In actuality, women have a limited say: if they do not agree, they return to court to face the judge, who may revoke supervision. Even when women return to court for new charges or because they refused to comply with sanctions, Gender Responsive County officers may recommend treatment to judges. If the judge agrees, a woman may continue with existing programming or attend other treatment programs. In Traditional County, judges usually order any programming, and the supervising officer is expected to implement the order. Compared to Traditional County officers, those in Gender Responsive County exert more influence on the programs women attend, on sanctions, and on court actions.

I did find evidence of differences in supervising officers' goals in the data. Traditional County supervising officers try to move women to the lowest level of supervision, or even eliminate supervision, as quickly as possible. They accomplish this by concentrating on whether women have met court-stipulated conditions, like paying supervision fees and restitution and doing community service work. Treatment comes into play mostly as a condition set by the judge. The goal of Gender Responsive County officers is also to ensure that women meet conditions. More-complex additional goals include figuring out the root and current causes of illegal behavior, linking women to resources, and setting requirements to address underlying causes. Gender Responsive County supervising officers invest considerable time and effort assessing women's various needs and arranging for programming to meet those needs.

The counties differ in other ways as well. Only women officers supervise the Gender Responsive County women offenders. The officers work as a team, which initially matches women to supervising officers based on the fit between a woman's needs and the officer's capabilities. Some officers specialize in working with women with limited cognitive ability. Others focus on women addicted to drugs. In Gender Responsive County, women's supervising officers only rarely change, usually when an officer leaves her job, or the team determines that a different officer can better meet a woman's needs. In Traditional County, both male and female supervising officers handle mixed-sex caseloads. They do not focus on meeting gender-related needs. Because Traditional County assignments depend on geographic location, supervising officers change when women move between zip codes. Case notes and research forms completed by supervising officers show that even when women do not move, they are commonly assigned to a new Traditional County officer during their year of supervision.

SERVICES, AGENCIES, AND PROGRAMS:
THE BROADER CONTEXT

Essential to understanding the women offenders who are this book's focus is the recognition that they are not confined to neighborhoods where they live, socialize, seek and receive services, and work. They navigate a wide array of geographically scattered county, regional, and state services and agencies. Bloom et al. (2003) note the challenge this poses for women offenders. The myriad of programs may be fragmented and distant, have conflicting requirements, or interfere with keeping supervision appointments. In the counties studied, women were sometimes served by multiple agencies and programs due to the supervising officers' referrals or requirements or, less often, those of a judge. Lawyers encouraged women to participate in particular programs before a court hearing, to demonstrate commitment to receiving help in the community. Women also connected to multiple programs due to family members' and friends' referrals and suggestions, fliers in jail, or personal searches for assistance.

The community setting in my research differs from the limited geographic areas observed in studies of women offenders in demarcated neighborhoods in large urban areas (e.g., Maher 2000; Miller 1986). The setting for this study is a broader, less personal, and less geographically limited community. The women frequently travel both inside and outside their counties of residence. They move between counties or even out of state. Given their mobility, trying to study these women by focusing on a single neighborhood makes it impossible to understand their lives.

The program environment includes various correctional programs, organizations and subsidies that help women obtain housing, state agencies for assisting children and their families, treatment programs, and other specialized programs. Women also become involved with medical insurance providers that cover expenses for physical and mental illness as well as substance abuse treatment.

Correctional Facilities and Monitoring

The state operates a women's prison, which offers an array of educational, training, treatment, and self-help programs. A pre-release, therapeutic drug-treatment program for women occupies one wing of a mixed-sex state prison. Each county contains a jail and an adjacent work release center. The jails in both counties house substance abuse treatment programs called the Intensive Drug Treatment Program. Despite the shared name, the county programs differ. In both counties, women live in the jail, the work release center, or the community while receiving substance abuse services. However, in Gender Responsive County, the Intensive Drug Treatment Program is for women only, whereas in Traditional County it serves men, too.

Gender Responsive County funds a program that combines electronically monitored house arrest and outpatient treatment for substance abuse. The program delivers rehabilitation and punishment for offenders who previously failed other substance abuse programs or who have probation or parole violations related to substance abuse. For the first fourteen weeks, participants "wear the bracelet" (are monitored electronically), attend treatment meetings three times a week, and take drug and alcohol tests. They must participate in at least two additional self-help meetings a week and seek work. Over time, monitoring and treatment requirements decrease, and women are "off the bracelet." In a second fourteen-week phase, participants attend treatment meetings and continue drug testing. If participants relapse or violate travel and living restrictions, the frequency of drug tests increases, and the women go back "on the bracelet," lose privileges, or are jailed. Gender Responsive County women often begin the Intensive Drug Treatment Program while living in jail or the work release center, and they continue with outpatient treatment and electronic surveillance as they move into the community.

During office and home visits, supervising officers are authorized to administer a urine analysis test for drugs, or a breath test for alcohol. They can even take women into custody in more public settings, and transport them to the jail or the supervision office for testing. After receiving a written release from women in substance abuse treatment, officers frequently rely on the treatment programs for mail or phone reports about test results. The jails, work release centers, and the Intensive Drug Treatment Program also may communicate test results to supervising officers.

The many requirements, programs, and agencies the women may face support Bloom et al.'s (2003) concerns about women's contending with multiple sources of help. Women offenders with numerous challenges must meet the requirements of a diverse set of programs, follow up on referrals, and find the help they need. Some are involved on a daily basis with multiple arms of this network. Getting to and attending correctional programs, submitting to tests, and accessing services can consume most or all of a woman's day. As I looked into the range of available programs and services, I saw the potential for fragmentation and the gaps even more clearly.

Housing

In addition to government subsidized and public housing, women in both counties have access to Oxford Houses and transitional housing. Oxford Houses are residential units where multiple people live in an affordable, self-help community after leaving residential substance abuse treatment (Dvorchak et al. 1995; Ferrari et al. 1999; Jason et al. 2001). Established by a nonprofit corporation, they exist in several states. Completion of a community, prison, or jail substance abuse treatment program establishes eligibility to live in an Oxford House. The Oxford Houses in or near the two counties of this study accommodate children. They use a democratic system of self-governance designed to empower women and help them become independent and assertive.

In both counties, transitional housing is another option for offenders leaving prisons and jails. Homeless shelters also accept women, but most have time limitations or are open only in the winter. Similarly, battered women's shelters provide temporary housing, but for a fairly limited time.

Aside from these options, when there were no other alternatives, some women in each county spent time at the county work release center as paying boarders.

The Child and Family Services Agency

The state Child and Family Services Agency investigates complaints of child endangerment, neglect, and abuse (referred to collectively as *child maltreatment* in this book); oversees visitation for children not in their mother's custody; arranges and manages foster care, including care by relatives; and handles family reunification. Although nine women in the study faced charges limited to child maltreatment, many others were charged with child maltreatment as well as other offenses. When women use drugs, reports from relatives or landlords often spark investigations by the agency. Incarcerated women usually lose child custody. Child and Family Services workers maintain contact with mothers who have children in foster care, and provide counseling and referrals to women who seek to regain custody. The agency requires mothers seeking custody to attend parenting classes or other specialized programs. Mothers must also proceed through the steps of brief supervised visits, overnight stays, and transfer of care and custody. In some cases, the Child and Family Services Agency stipulates a substance abuse evaluation and treatment before women can regain visitation privileges or custody. The requirements of community supervision may substantially overlap with those for keeping or getting child visitation privileges and custody.

Substance Abuse Treatment and Medical Insurance

Substance abuse evaluation services, detoxification programs (referred to as detox), residential treatment programs, outpatient treatment programs, education programs, and self-help groups are available to women who use illicit drugs or abuse alcohol. Aside from Community Mental Health Agency counseling and groups, six other local substance abuse treatment programs deliver outpatient or residential services. Women also apply to residential treatment programs located outside the counties. The residential programs and some outpatient programs accept women from either of the two counties.

Medical insurance affects access to substance abuse treatment, mental health care, and other medical services. At the time of the study, a statewide demonstration Medicaid program had successfully expanded eligibility, prioritized health care benefits, restricted benefits in nonpriority areas, and managed participants' care. Managed health care designates particular health plans, dental care organizations, and mental health organizations to assess the needs of women and direct them to approved medical resources. Of particular importance for women under supervision, the benefits package covers mental health, chemical dependency, and dental services. Eligibility is granted to people at 100 percent of the poverty level set by the federal government. Premiums are set on a sliding scale, and past due premiums can be waived in certain circumstances, including homelessness. An evaluation determined that the state insurance program increased access to substance abuse and mental health services. Despite the significant resources delivered by state insurance, there are barriers due to enrollment delays. Also, some women cannot access services until they pay past-due premiums or copayments. Others must wait until a new calendar year begins.

Other Programs and Services

Some programs for women offenders operate in just one county. Traditional County delivers an HIV/AIDS awareness and education program within the community corrections department. Nearly all women on probation and parole must attend the sessions. In Gender Responsive County, the Community Corrections Agency contracts with professionals to run three different types of specialized, women-only groups for self-esteem, grief counseling, and support. The women's support group focuses on life skills, such as résumé preparation and money management. Also, during designated hours each week, the state employment agency counselor works at the Gender Responsive County community corrections building. She provides employment testing and counseling services to women under supervision.

Women may access services and programs not specifically designed for offenders as a result of a referral by the supervising officer, at the suggestion of another person, or through their own initiative. Some services already mentioned include: employment, alcohol, and drug treatment programs; shelters; the Child and Family Services Agency; and the state insurance program. Other available services and programs are mental health care, dual diagnosis treatment (for people with both substance abuse and other mental health problems), medical care, domestic violence programs, and educational programs ranging from GED preparation to college courses. Women may receive food stamps or other public benefits from the welfare agency, and a few receive workers' compensation for injury or unemployment benefits, which are all unrelated to offender status.

THE SAMPLE

I located the Gender Responsive County community supervision program through a national study of innovative and promising approaches for women offenders (Morash, Bynum, and Koons 1996). It fit the criteria identified in the literature and in interviews with numerous experts about the most effective gender-responsive practices for women offenders. I later selected Traditional County, an adjacent jurisdiction with a more typical approach to supervision for women, for comparison.

The two counties' demographic differences are summarized in table 1.1. Gender Responsive County's population is larger, its annual median income is higher, and a smaller proportion of its households live in poverty. It has a very high proportion of white residents, and its proportion of Hispanics is lower than Traditional County's. In general, Gender Responsive County residents earn more money, and more racial and ethnic minorities reside in Traditional County.

The 2000 U.S. Census, conducted close to the data collection period, shows similarities in county density (about 180 and 240 people per square mile for Gender Responsive and Traditional Counties, respectively) and a mix of small cities, suburban areas, and rural areas. In 2000, the index person (murder and nonnegligent manslaughter, robbery, forcible rape, and aggravated assault) rate was lower in Gender Responsive County than in Traditional County (approximately 153 versus 418 crimes reported, per 10,000 people in the population). The property offense rate also was lower in Gender Responsive County (approximately 434 versus 850, per 10,000 people for burglary, larceny and theft, motor vehicle theft, and arson). Differences in crime rates and resource levels could explain why Gender Responsive County developed and supported a unique approach to probation and parole for women. However, these differences do not negate findings about the impact of different approaches to supervision, particularly since women with similar backgrounds were compared across the two counties.

TABLE 1.1. *Approximate county characteristics from the 2000 census*

County characteristics	County	
	gender responsive	traditional
	pop. over 330,000	pop. over 280,000
Race (percent)		
White	91	82
Black/African American	1	1
American Indian	1	1
Asian	3	2
Other race	2	11
Multiple races	2	3
Hispanic or Latina (percent)	5	17
Families below poverty level (percent)	5	10
Median household income	over $50,000	about $40,000

Note: To maintain the women's confidentiality, the numbers are approximate.

From 1997 to 1999, the research staff attempted to sample all women coming onto probation or parole caseloads in the two counties. To be eligible for the study, women had to have been convicted of at least one felony. The sampling protocol included women transferring in from other counties and states. Table 1.2 provides the numbers of women we attempted to and actually did include in the study. Two sets of circumstances led to omitting women from the sample. Some women transferred immediately to another state or county and could not be tracked; others were not interviewed and lacked case notes. The research staff obtained data for a higher proportion of women in Gender Responsive County than in Traditional County. This may be because Gender Responsive County officers helped more with contacting women to schedule interviews and provided case notes for more women.

Although the research staff used several means (phone calls, visits, and letters), they depended heavily on supervising officers for contact with women and access to data. When supervising officers lost contact with women, the research staff often lost contact, too. Dropping women from

TABLE 1.2. *Proportion of sample included in the study*

	Percent (and number) by county		
Inclusion in study	gender responsive (N = 186)	traditional (N = 253)	combined (N = 439)
Not included	10.2 (19)	20.2 (51)	15.9 (70)
Included	89.8 (167)	79.8 (202)	84.1 (369)

the study who broke contact with supervising officers would bias the data toward those who complied with supervision, at least to the point of staying in touch. There is no easy solution to lost contact with frequently moving and sometimes evasive women on probation and parole. O'Brien (2001), for instance, started her research on Illinois women on parole with fifty-five subjects, but she was able to complete five planned interviews for only 36 percent of the total number of women. She concentrates on those twenty women in order to understand their experiences after leaving prison. My strategy is different. I combined information from every available data source on each woman. Women with partial data are included in the analysis. Table 1.3 presents information on the proportion of women with each type of data.

The study sample includes just three Asian women, but data exist for several Hispanic, Native American, and African American women (see table 1.4). Official records identify all but one Hispanic woman as Caucasian or "other," not African American, Native American, or Asian, and that woman described herself as Native American and Hispanic. In spite of the small numbers of Native Americans and African Americans in both counties, these groups are overrepresented in comparison to both counties' demographics. The sample somewhat underrepresents white and Hispanic women and greatly underrepresents Asians. As a result, the sample has a higher proportion of Native American and African American women than the population does.

Similar percentages of women in both counties entered the study just after serving time in prison or jail. The numbers are 19.2 percent in Gender Responsive County and 12.9 percent in Traditional County. Prisons can provide helpful programming, but they also can create problems by sepa-

TABLE 1.3. *Type of data available for study subjects*

Type of data	Percent (and number) of women with each type of data by county		
	gender responsive	traditional	combined
First interview with woman	65.9 (110)	66.8 (135)	66.4 (245)
Follow-up interview with woman	69.5 (116)	45.5 (92)	56.4 (208)
First staff survey	87.4 (146)	81.2 (164)	84.0 (310)
Follow-up staff survey	88.6 (148)	79.2 (160)	83.5 (308)
Case notes	100.0 (167)	100.0 (202)	100.0 (369)
Official record check	100.0 (167)	100.0 (202)	100.0 (369)
Total	100.0 (167)	100.0 (202)	100.0 (369)

rating women from their children and community resources. The women in the two counties start out similar in terms of the positive and negative results of incarceration. Thus, county differences in outcomes cannot be explained by initial variation in whether the women were just released.

THE DATA

For each woman, I combined data from all available sources into qualitative case information. There are six possible data sources for each case. Two sources of information were interviews attempted with each woman, one at the beginning of the year of supervision and the other, a follow-up interview, at the year's end. Third, supervising officers turned in an initial form for each woman, assessing her needs and perception of the justness of her sentence. Fourth, the officers participated in a follow-up survey after supervising the women for a year, giving information about the help provided, referrals for specific problems, and outcomes. Fifth, supervising officers maintained chronological case notes in a database. The first entry included information about risk score, supervision level, any reasons for a difference between the level of supervision and the corresponding risk-score level, and intake interview results. And sixth, research staff gathered information from a state correctional department electronic file of results

TABLE 1.4. *Race and ethnicity of women in the study*

	Percent (and number) by county		
	---	---	---
Race and ethnicity	gender responsive (N = 167)	traditional (N = 202)	combined (N = 369)
White/Caucasian	88.6 (148)	89.1 (180)	88.9 (328)
Native American	4.8 (8)	6.9 (14)	6.0 (22)
Black/African American	5.4 (9)	3.5 (7)	4.3 (16)
Asian	1.2 (2)	0.5 (1)	0.8 (3)
Not Hispanic	92.8 (155)	87.6 (177)	90.0 (332)
Hispanic	7.2 (12)	12.4 (25)	10.0 (37)

of drug tests conducted by jails, work release centers, and supervising officers before and after the year of supervision. They also gathered information from this file on prior and new convictions, periods in jail and prison, and participation in treatment programs. Combining all available data, I created 369 cases and stored and analyzed them with N6 software, developed by QSR International.

Throughout the book, I indicate that the data source is an interview with a woman by references such as "the woman said" or "the woman told the interviewer." I identify data from supervising officers' survey forms with phrases such as "research forms turned in" or "research forms filled out" by supervising officers. I indicate that information comes from case notes with phrases such as "supervising officers noted" and "supervising officers wrote." Supervising officers' case notes provided any information attributed to the supervising officer, police, or professionals who worked with women. Appendixes A and B include the survey and interview questions.

Compared to Traditional County supervising officers, those in Gender Responsive County generated more copious chronological case notes. The Gender Responsive County officers explained why women broke laws or used drugs. They often described the women's emotions, such as their fears, embarrassment, and grief. The officers gave detailed information on conversations with women and their family members, as well as with program and agency staff members. Sometimes the notes convey the supervising officers' sense of urgency about getting drug users off drugs and off the streets before they harm or even kill themselves. The Traditional County officers produced leaner notes, focused primarily on whether women met the conditions of parole and probation. With few exceptions, Traditional County notes read like a chronicle of events, detached from supervising officers' reactions or actions. Early on, I concluded that the case notes reflected real differences between supervision in the two counties. I validated the differences through additional analysis of other data sources, especially the interviews with women.

I took several steps to preserve study participants' confidentiality. I use pseudonyms throughout the book. I do not precisely describe unusual offenses, job circumstances, or life events. I omit or slightly alter details of children's ages or sexes. Table 1.1 contains rounded numbers reflecting county demographics; the text contains rounded numbers for crime rates. I also omit references to the state medical insurance program evaluation.

The text refers to, describes, or quotes nearly 200 of the 369 women in the sample. I give pseudonyms to the women mentioned multiple times in the book and to women about whom I provide detailed information. Pseudonyms remind us that the book is about individuals, not cases or numbers. Pseudonyms also link information on the same woman within and between chapters. To reduce the confusion produced by using many names, I refer to women mentioned only briefly without giving them pseudonyms. Consistent with the book's aim to highlight both the common and unique experiences of women on probation and parole, examples pertain to many different women, not a small number of unique cases.

DATA CODING AND ANALYSIS

I started the analysis by coding the qualitative data on numerous dimensions, to reflect women's situations and circumstances, their experiences on probation and parole, and their outcomes. Repeated readings of the data suggested specific coding themes and variants of those themes. Good qualitative research requires examining the coding scheme for possible omission of key themes. For example, after examining the coding scheme early in the analysis, I saw that the codes captured women's many disadvantages, but not their advantages. At this point, I reexamined all the data and coded for advantages. The list was short, but I did not ignore themes that I had initially overlooked.

At first, I tried to make sense of key themes in the cases by considering all women and then comparing women in the two counties. I could not clearly demonstrate county differences, connections between women's needs and supervision experiences, or reasons for success or failure. After multiple readings of case data, I realized that the organization of the women's past and current illegal activity profoundly influences their circumstances, supervision, and outcomes. In the rest of the analysis, I treated the concept that I refer to as *dominant illegal activity* as a central idea to consider in relation to women's needs, supervision, and outcomes. Women's dominant illegal activity affects their behaviors and the reactions of supervising officers and other people. It explains where women live, how often they move, and their connections to their intimate partners and children. Because of the importance of the concept, I restarted the analysis with a new strategy of making comparisons within and between dominant illegal activity subgroups. The importance of women's dominant criminal activity is the reason for devoting chapters 2 and 3 to describing the illegal activity subgroups of women and their characteristics. It also is the reason for examining county differences for each subgroup separately in chapters 4 through 6.

The literature establishes the importance of the intersections of gender, race, ethnicity, social class, sexual orientation, and other markers of social location to explaining a person's life course, resources, and opportunities (Morash 2006, 3–4). It shows how such intersections affect the responses of the justice system (Morash 2006, 231–32). Recognizing the impact of these intersections, I examine race and ethnicity in relation to women's patterns of illegal activity, their backgrounds and situations, and their experience and outcomes of supervision. Unfortunately, this analysis is limited by the very few women who identified themselves as lesbians, and the predominance of white women who are not of Hispanic origin in the sample. However, to the degree possible, I pay attention to any unique characteristics and supervision experiences of African American, Native American, and Hispanic women.

I use several methods to increase the credibility of conclusions. One is to establish consistent information within a case, whenever there are two or more information sources, and to use the best available information if there is a discrepancy. For example, some women's case notes and official records show no illegal activity during the year, but they told interviewers they supported themselves by dealing drugs, through prostitution, or by committing other crimes. They are coded as committing new offenses.

I also maintain credibility by examining the detailed case information before finalizing my conclusions. For example, one woman identified Alcoholics Anonymous as the program that helped her the most, but when asked why it was helpful, she briefly responded that it was "noncommittal." This specific information about program experiences gave me crucial insight into the reason for the woman's continued criminal activity: she continued to break the law during the year because of minimal engagement in the program she described as "helpful."

Challenging initial conclusions by studying negative cases serves as a third way to ensure credibility. Negative cases do not always lead to rejecting findings as invalid. They sometimes generate new findings, in the form of more fully developed explanations. For example, the style of supervision in Gender Responsive County seemed to push active drug users into substance abuse treatment, especially in the Intensive Drug Treatment Program and private residential programs. This in turn led to positive changes, such as getting a job. After I discovered this common Gender Responsive County pattern, I systematically assessed whether the same pattern ever occurred in Traditional County. Specifically, I tested the idea that Gender Responsive County promotes positive change by pressuring women to get intensive drug treatment. I found that Traditional County cases do not follow the same pattern. Some Traditional County women make positive changes after entering treatment. However, the supervising officers do not provide the impetus for starting treatment. For instance, one woman's relatives pressured her to enter treatment. Conclusions presented throughout the book emphasize typical patterns, but also point to and explain alternative and contradictory patterns.

As a final way to establish the credibility of conclusions, I analyzed county differences separately for each subgroup. For the large subgroup of women who entered the criminal justice system primarily because of their drug use, I also compared the counties separately for the women who failed and those who succeeded. I consider discoveries of the same county differences across multiple subgroups as evidence of valid findings.

CONCLUSION

The remainder of this book reflects the puzzle-like fit between women's dominant criminal activity, their needs and circumstances, and how they fared on probation and parole. Part 1 describes the dominant illegal activity subgroups of women on probation and parole, and part 2 connects the type of supervision—gender-responsive or traditional—to what happened to each subgroup during a year of supervision. The concluding chapter revisits the promise and the potentially negative consequences of gender-responsive supervision for women, and makes recommendations for research, practice, and policy.

I

THE WOMEN
ON PROBATION
AND PAROLE

2

Dominant Crimes

My problem's not drugs or alcohol. It's anger.
CASSANDRA, Traditional County

Cassandra, whose comment opens this chapter, recognizes that women on probation and parole are not a homogeneous group. She was repeatedly convicted for assaultive behavior, but she knows that other women who break the law are substance abusers. She sees their patterns of crime as different from her own.

Early in my work with the data, I also saw distinct subgroups of women on the county caseloads who engaged in different dominant illegal activities. The subgroup distinctions are crucial to making sense of the women's experiences on probation or parole. The supervising officers' tactics and the women's actions must be analyzed and understood in relation to dominant illegal activity. The signs of women's success are related to dominant illegal activity. For example, leaving an intimate partner signifies success for women whose crimes result from partners' demands or persuasion. Alternatively, for women who break the law because they are addicted to drugs, success equates to overcoming addiction. The two counties can be meaningfully compared only when separate assessments are developed for the different subgroups. I also had to consider the outcomes of most importance to each subgroup to make relevant comparisons.

It was fairly easy to identify the dominant crime for most women. The proportions of women in each category were very similar for the two counties (see table 2.1). Almost two-thirds of the women's dominant crimes were substance-centered. Possessing illegal substances and committing economic offenses to earn money to purchase drugs dominated their crimes. Because my initial analysis showed no background, supervision, or outcome difference between women who abuse alcohol only and the much larger proportion that uses other drugs, I combined women with alcohol and drug problems.

TABLE 2.1. *Dominant crime subgroups of women in the study*

	Percent (and number) by county		
Dominant crime	gender responsive (N = 167)	traditional (N = 202)	combined (N = 369)
Substance-centered	65.3 (109)	65.3 (132)	65.3 (241)
Economic only	22.2 (37)	12.9 (26)	17.1 (63)
Violence-involved	2.4 (4)	4.5 (9)	3.5 (13)
Marijuana cultivation	5.4 (9)	1.5 (3)	3.3 (12)
Child maltreatment	1.2 (2)	3.5 (7)	2.4 (9)
Partner-influenced	1.8 (3)	1.5 (3)	1.6 (6)
Drug manufacture and trade	0.0	1.5 (3)	0.8 (3)
Died during study	0.0	1.5 (3)	0.8 (3)
Felony driving offenses	0.6 (1)	0.5 (1)	0.5 (2)
Unclear	1.2 (2)	7.4 (15)	4.6 (17)

Economic-only offenders who committed crimes such as embezzlement, shoplifting, and welfare fraud constituted the next largest subgroup. For the two counties, 17.1 percent of the women were economic-only offenders. Drug and alcohol addictions did not drive the economic offenders: many had never tried any illegal substance, while others used marijuana or alcohol only sporadically or had stopped using drugs after their teen years.

Less than five percent of the women had crimes dominated by violence; marijuana cultivation; child maltreatment; aiding and abetting a male partner (called *partner-influenced*); or drug manufacture, distribution, and selling. Violence might be one-time or repeated. Women who broke the law only by aiding criminal intimate partners or by maltreating children made up a small part of probation and parole caseloads. Just two women were convicted for felony driving offenses alone. Three women died during the study year, and insufficient information made it impossible to determine the dominant illegal activity of seventeen women (4.6 percent).

SUBSTANCE-CENTERED WOMEN

Mary Anne, most recently convicted for possessing a controlled substance, exemplifies substance-centered women. She first used marijuana, amphetamines, and speed at age fourteen, and crack at eighteen. Her history of convictions resulted from theft, two probation violations, and possessing a controlled substance. At thirty-six, Mary Anne's most recent arrest was for shoplifting at a discount grocery store. During the arrest, the police searched her and found a baggie full of methamphetamines in her purse. During the year of supervision, she tested positive for methamphetamine use. Although her criminal history includes probation violations and shoplifting, these all result from drug use.

Mary Anne's story is typical of the women that another researcher referred to as "street women" (Daly 1992, 14). Locating similar findings across studies confirms the validity of qualitative research. The women I call *substance-centered* resemble Daly's street women. In both my study and Daly's research, women who are regular users of drugs like methamphetamines, cocaine, heroin, and extreme amounts of alcohol also forge checks, use stolen credit cards, engage in prostitution, and make and sell drugs. The women use illegal means to generate income for basic living expenses and to purchase drugs for themselves and sometimes for their partners. Other studies confirm the link between drug use and property crimes for economic gain (Anglin and Speckart 1988; Fagan 1994; Goode 1997; Griffin and Armstrong 2003; Horney, Osgood, and Marshall 1995; Needle and Mills 1994; Nurco et al. 1988; Uggen and Thompson 2003). In addition to committing economic offenses, substance-centered women commonly drive without a license or in a stolen car, either because their driving privileges have been revoked or because they cannot afford a license, insurance, or car. Exposing their children to illegal drugs and paraphernalia, like needles and pipes, leads to convictions for child maltreatment. In my sample of substance-centered women, the earliest juvenile delinquency histories began at age ten, and the most serious adult justice system history was five incarcerations. Despite the many different crimes committed, the substance-centered women's interview responses and case notes confirm substance use as central to their illegal activity. Substance use profoundly affects not only criminal behavior, but also work and living arrangements, relationships with intimate partners, and contact with children.

Substance-centered women rarely committed violent acts. Only a few of the many women in this subgroup possessed a firearm, and none had shot another person. A few have restraining orders or a prior arrest for assault for fighting with an intimate partner. One woman with three prior assault convictions recently broke the nose of her ex-partner's new partner during a fight. Another was present when an associate shot another person during a drug deal. These incidents constitute the small number of out-of-the-ordinary acts of violence committed by substance-centered women.

Substance-centered women do not share a common drug use history, except for their high drug consumption levels. Even the woman with the lowest level of use had consumed methamphetamines daily for two years. The two women who started using alcohol and marijuana earliest began when they were three and five years old, respectively. Others began to use drugs as preteens, teenagers, young adults, or older adults. Women who used before or during their teenage years had tried a great variety of drugs — including marijuana, alcohol, methamphetamines, LSD, barbiturates, crack in various forms, and heroin. In general, women who used after age eighteen specialized in methamphetamines, cocaine, heroin, or a combination of these.

Among the substance-centered women, three distinct groups are differentiated by their point on a trajectory to recovery. Women in the "failing" group actively used drugs and had at least one additional problem. They absconded, committed new crimes, or ended the year incarcerated. Those "making it" still used drugs but avoided absconding, reincarceration, and new crimes, other than drug possession and consumption. Despite substantial substance use histories, the "beyond use" group abstained from drugs before supervision began, did not abscond or commit new offenses, and lived in the community at year's end.

I used information from several sources to categorize women as substance-centered and to determine whether they were failing, making it, or beyond use. Supervising officers recorded admissions of use, test results, reports from relatives and treatment professionals, and their own observations of women. Women also volunteered information in response to a lengthy set of interview questions about drugs.

For the substance-centered women, the available evidence led me to categorize nearly identical proportions in each county as beyond drug use (see table 2.2). At the end of the supervision year, I classified a slightly higher proportion of women in Traditional County than those in Gender Responsive County as failing and the situation was reversed for women who were making it.

TABLE 2.2. *Subgroups of substance-centered women in the study*

	Percent (and number) by county		
Drug use and outcome	gender responsive (N = 109)	traditional (N = 132)	combined (N = 241)
Using drugs, failing	42.2 (46)	46.2 (61)	44.4 (107)
Using drugs, making it	37.6 (41)	31.8 (42)	34.4 (83)
Beyond drug use	20.2 (22)	22.0 (29)	21.2 (51)

Two key bodies of literature examine the behavior of substance-centered women. In recent years, scientific studies have revealed that repeated use of some drugs results in negative physical effects on the brain (Leshner 1997; Logan et al. 2002). Physical effects combined with recollection of positive feelings associated with drug use trigger the desire to use again. Compared to men who use drugs, women are especially vulnerable to some physiological effects of substance use, which is more frequently a product of traumatic life events and psychiatric disorders, such as anxiety and depression (Briere et al. 1997; Brady and Ashley 2005, 1; Logan et al. 2002). Even before brain and cognitive science advances, phenomenological research described the power of drug and alcohol addiction and dependence in similar terms. Trying to capture the essence of addiction, Peele writes: "We decide the person is addicted when he [or she] acts addicted: when he [or she] pursues a drug's effects no matter what the negative consequences for his [or her] life" (1985, 18). Substance-centered women act with agency, but the biological, personal, and social experiences associated with addiction and dependence severely constrain their choices and actions. I refer to the women as substance-centered to highlight the apparent force of drugs and alcohol in their lives.

WOMEN INVOLVED IN VIOLENCE

Most women (seven of thirteen, or 53.8 percent) whose illegal activity was primarily violent acted just once against another person, out of anger. Examples of one-time offenses are: throwing a firebomb into another woman's yard over an outstanding debt; assaulting a woman because she dated an ex-boyfriend; and shooting a gun into the ground during an argument with a teenage son.

Unlike women who acted violently once in anger, two women belonged to groups with violence-supporting norms and values. Deborah and her coworkers abused several children and caused the death of one. Cassandra's family, including her father and several siblings, had assault convictions. She also belonged to a gang that repeatedly got into fights. Cassandra's assaults on two girls she described as "former best friends" brought her into the justice system. During the study year, she jumped over a jewelry counter at a department store and attacked her cousin, an employee at the store.

Of the thirteen violence-involved women, the remaining four engaged in assaultive behavior related to mental illness, their own victimization, or substance use. For instance, Samantha used and sold cocaine. The courts convicted her for stabbing her boyfriend in the throat with a knife. Samantha said she acted in self-defense when her boyfriend tried to rape her. The police report attributed the incident to an argument about another woman. Immediately after the incident, Samantha slashed her wrists. During her supervision, Samantha assaulted her girlfriend in what the supervising officer described as "a lover's spat that got violent." Anna, another violent woman with complex problems, stabbed her husband. She described him as "mentally abusive and cruel," but the connection between his abuse and the stabbing is unclear. Preceding the incident, Anna had stopped taking medication for bipolar disorder and consumed ten alcoholic drinks. She asked her husband whether he wanted to see how she would retaliate against neighbors, and then cut his arm to demonstrate. She immediately called the police to report the attack. For women like Samantha and Anna, violent acts stand out as the dominant influence in their convictions and continued lawbreaking. However, their situations are complicated by their own victimization, mental illness, or alcohol use. The violence-involved women lack histories of continuous drug use, addiction, and dependence. They sometimes act violently when drinking, but at other times there is no connection between their drinking and violence.

WOMEN INFLUENCED BY PARTNERS

Six women broke the law as a result of associations and relationships with men. Although they did not use illegal drugs or have alcohol problems, these women aided, abetted, and lived with partners who did. One partner-influenced woman, Peg, told the interviewer that her boyfriend physically attacked her about twice a week and had recently dislocated her jaw. He taught Peg to alter checks, which resulted in her conviction. After the police apprehended Peg for trying to cash an altered check in a grocery store, they searched her boyfriend's van and discovered his drugs. Peg admitted to the drug possession and forgery so her boyfriend would not beat her; he wanted to avoid a third felony conviction and a prison sentence.

Kimberly's illegal actions show several ways that partners may compel women to break the law. She drove her husband to a shopping area parking lot so he could steal a woman's purse, and had previously passed a stolen check so he could buy drugs. Earlier she had been convicted for hindering prosecution, for lying to police about her former husband's whereabouts. Although Kimberly tried various drugs as a teenager, she had not used for over a decade. She had no juvenile record, and no record of positive drug tests or drug-related arrests. If not for the pressures exerted by her partners, she probably would not have broken the law.

At the suggestion or insistence of partners, women sometimes commit economic crimes. They are present when police find their partners' drugs in vehicles and at their residences. Relationships with abusive men and connections between men and the women's crimes repeat a pattern of entrapment that Richie (1996) described for women jailed in Cook County, Illinois. Unlike substance-centered women, whose partners influence them to break the law, women in the partner-influenced subgroup do not use drugs themselves.

REPEAT ECONOMIC OFFENDERS

Very few women (fifteen, or 4.1 percent) repeatedly committed only economic crimes. This subgroup rarely used drugs, and any drug history was unrelated to their economic crimes. Characteristic histories are: multiple shoplifting convictions; continuous involvement in a criminal group that steals, receives, and resells goods; and forgery or embezzlement convictions. One woman had a history of embezzling from employers that extended for more than twenty years. Another was arrested for grand theft as a juvenile. Economic crimes may be substantial, because they are repeated or involve thousands or even hundreds of thousands of dollars.

The repeat economic offenders differ from each other depending on their social standing, which determines their access to money or goods to steal or sell. Women in the most advantaged economic situations steal from their employers. However, conviction almost always reduces their initial economic advantage. Before her year of supervision, one repeat economic offender worked part time in a law office and supplemented her income by forging checks. Just before she stopped going to work, she convinced her employer to pay her rent by promising to pay him back with her next paycheck. At the same time, she signed a contract to purchase a car with monthly payments, and kept the car but made no payments. Without the supervising officer's permission, she moved frequently. At one point during the year, she relocated to another state and was convicted there on a new charge of grand larceny. Demonstrating a similar pattern of repeat offenses, Helene, who had embezzled from a former employer, obtained a new job where she stole over $20,000. After the supervising officer banned Helene from any job that involved handling money, she worked as a loan officer. In the new position, she defrauded customers by telling them that denied loans had been approved, which spurred them to make purchases they could not afford. Helene's misrepresentation of the loans did not benefit her financially. Repeat economic offenders who steal from employers reveal a pattern of dishonesty that, at least for some, is not even related to clear economic gain.

Instead of stealing from employers, unemployed women commit welfare fraud, promote and profit from others' prostitution, forge checks, steal, or sell stolen goods. Some steal from their relatives. The opportunities available lead repeat economic offenders to illegal means to improve their material well-being.

ONE-TIME ECONOMIC OFFENDERS

The forty-eight one-time economic offenders make up 13 percent of women in the study. They steal to obtain necessities, help their families during tough times, or acquire unaffordable luxuries. Struggling with poverty, the most disadvantaged women inaccurately reported their incomes in order to fraudulently obtain food stamps, welfare support, or state medical insurance. Facing a family financial crisis, one woman embezzled from her employer to cover $50,000 in medical expenses for her uninsured husband. To satisfy her desire for luxuries, another woman stole a piece of jewelry from the shop where she worked. Like the repeat economic offenders, the poorest steal from public benefit systems, and those who are better off steal from employers.

MARIJUANA CULTIVATORS

Women grow marijuana for recreational use, to treat their own aches and pains, or to distribute it to other people for medicinal purposes. For those who use marijuana themselves, the drug use does not permeate their lives as it does for substance-centered women. If they had ever used drugs other than marijuana and alcohol, which was only the case for a few of them, the marijuana cultivators stopped several years before the research period. None had the long histories of early use of many drugs that characterized many substance-centered women. All were on probation for the first time. Marijuana's more limited impact compared to other drugs is seen in the women's lifestyles, described more fully in the next chapter, and in the positive year-end outcome for all of them.

WOMEN WHO MISTREAT CHILDREN

The nine women with illegal activity limited to child maltreatment differ from each other in their specific acts. Roxanne said the child neglect charge against her and her husband resulted from an inability to maintain a clean house while they were physically ill. Marlee's neglect charge stemmed from a drug raid at the house where she and her child lived. One woman's estranged husband reported her for hitting their child so hard that she caused bruises. Women in this subgroup generally were charged with only one child maltreatment offense. Prior convictions — for instance, shoplifting — had no discernible connection to the child maltreatment charges and had occurred several years before.

OTHER WOMEN

Just three women who did not use illegal drugs themselves earned illegal income through drug manufacture, distribution, or selling. All three were on parole after spending time in prison. The first woman had married a drug dealer. For a second time, the police caught the couple with drugs and firearms in the home. It is unclear whether the woman was cooperating with her husband in the drug business or was just home when the raid happened. The second woman was convicted for possessing methamphetamines, packaging material, and a scale. The third sold drugs to generate income. She had used drugs only a few times over four years before her conviction. Information is very limited on the few women involved in the drug trade who were not users. Because I was unable to gain much insight into their backgrounds and supervision experiences, I do not discuss them in subsequent chapters.

Insufficient information also prevents me from writing about the women convicted of felony driving. One was charged with hit and run and reckless driving. Another said she was charged with "felony driving without a license."

Three substance-centered women in Traditional County died before the year ended. The case notes for Monica indicate low-level supervision, and mental health and substance abuse treatment on an outpatient basis. She committed suicide. Faye's drug use extended for several years. Her parole expired after a few months, so supervision was minimal. She also committed suicide before the year was up. With a history of suicide attempts, Heather had received mental health counseling for six years. After seventeen years of crack cocaine use, she continued to use during the year of supervision. At one point, she called her supervising officer to say that she was upset because she and her boyfriend were not getting along. She declined the supervising officer's offer to pick her up in his car and get her out of the boyfriend's residence, because she did not want her family to see her under the influence of drugs. Subsequently, the supervising officer "directed her to develop a support system and work on her spiritual life," and increased her required substance abuse treatment to two sessions a week. Soon after, the landlord discovered Heather had been brutally murdered in her home. Although I do not touch on these women's lives any further, I recognize their loss as a tragedy that might have been prevented through better understanding of addiction and recovery, or improved treatment or community supervision programming.

Insufficient information exists to categorize the seventeen remaining women into an illegal activity subgroup. They are concentrated in Traditional County, where case notes are brief, and the research staff experienced difficulty arranging interviews.

CONCLUSION

Grouping the women by dominant patterns of crime allows us to see that study participants reflect the national profile of women offenders. Consistent with statistics nationwide, two-thirds of women enter the justice system because they use drugs or alcohol (Langan and Pelissier 2001; Peters et al. 1997). Substance-centered women are involved in a constellation of different offenses, including economic crimes, prostitution, drug manufacture and dealing, and child maltreatment. Their crimes result from a lifestyle of heavy drug use and the need to pay for drugs.

Women who concentrate on economic crimes are the second largest subgroup. Most commit just one offense. A smaller number of repeat economic offenders steals from employers, stores, or public benefit programs. They display a pattern of repeated dishonesty and illegal methods to generate income.

Other dominant illegal activities constitute a very small proportion of probation and parole caseloads for women in this study. As is the case for the national population, violence-dominated crime patterns are not characteristic of women (Greenfeld and Snell 1999). Additionally, as other studies show, men typically exclude women from high-level drug dealing and organized criminal groups (Maher 2000), so this pattern of offending is rare for women.

The next chapter describes the characteristics, circumstances, and needs of each illegal activity subgroup. It will set the stage for the analysis of whether and how women's needs are addressed in Gender Responsive and Traditional Counties.

3

Women's Characteristics by Dominant Crime Subgroup

[Interviewer: "How could supervision be improved?"]
Addressing individual needs, not with a cookie cutter.
PEG, Traditional County

Women's dominant crimes are linked to their social location—their standing in existing social arrangements that depend on gender, race, and class—as well as to their often numerous and severe troubles. More specifically, the women in the different dominant crime subgroups vary in terms of length of involvement in illegal activity, education and employment, mental health or illness, and the resources and criminality of support networks. Women's criminal histories and social locations affect their resources. The subgroup differences lend support to Peg's statement above, that supervision must address individual needs.

As I note in the introduction, numerous previous studies document the problems and barriers that women offenders face. Building on those studies, this chapter contrasts women with different dominant crimes to show the complexity and intensity of their problems. Problem areas, like mental health, fully discussed elsewhere in the literature, receive fairly brief coverage. Instead, I give more attention to previously neglected problem areas in women's lives. One important issue described at length is repeated moves from one dangerous place to another by substance-centered women. Another is the nature of women's social networks. The descriptive information on each type of problem allows me to critically assess supervising officers' responses to women in part 2 of the book.

DEGREES OF DISADVANTAGE

Substance-centered women are the most chronically and fully disadvantaged. Violence-involved and partner-influenced women also suffer numerous hardships. Economic offenders, women charged with child mal-treatment, and marijuana cultivators experience fewer difficulties. Details about these women's lives show both the depth and variety of their prob-lems and exceptions within subgroups.

Extreme Disadvantages of Substance-Centered Women

Substance-centered women are especially likely to experience problems early in life, with negative ramifications that limit their resources and op-portunities for many years (Centers for Disease Control and Prevention 2005; Chesney-Lind 1997; Felitti et al. 1998). In particular, trauma from childhood victimization often leads to mental illness. Many substance-centered women told interviewers or supervising officers that they had been diagnosed as depressed. A subset also named one or more other diag-noses—including bipolar disorder, schizophrenia, and anxiety disorder—as well as the learning disability ADHD (attention deficit hyperactivity disor-der). "Self-medicating" with illegal substances initiates and perpetuates drug dependence and addiction (Ladwig and Andersen 1989; Vogt 1998). Analysis of quantitative data for the women in the current study showed that a sizable group had simultaneous needs related to substance abuse, emotional instability, and mental illness (Holtfreter and Morash 2003). The sections that follow are based on confirming qualitative data that reveal how drug use and the interrelated problems of trauma and mental illness combine to compromise health, education, employment, housing, social support networks, and child custody and care.

Disrupted Education and Workforce Participation. Drug use that starts at an early age and continues over time greatly limits women's education and capacity to find and keep good jobs. Most women who used drugs during the year of supervision failed to complete high school; some never even started high school. Few have technical training or have taken community college courses to prepare them for particular occupations. Education and training deficiencies place the vast majority of substance-centered women outside of or, at best, at the margins of the legitimate workforce. Most do not work at all. When they work, their pay is low and employment is spo-radic. Examples of typical jobs are baby-sitting for relatives in exchange for room and board, state-funded work caring for their own disabled parents, offering food samples at department stores, and seasonal work for logging companies, watching over trucks that have been loaded. A few women told interviewers they earned money by selling drugs, through prostitution, or by engaging in food stamp and welfare fraud. For a few, food stamps are the only income source. Public benefits rarely fully support women. In addition to the incompatibility of continued drug use and a legitimate job, disabilities, serious illnesses like hepatitis and heart disease, and dental problems (including no teeth) prevent women from working. No work or instability in employment, the inability to work, and little income are the norm.

Women who abstain from drugs succeeded just slightly more often in the workforce than active users. The most successful woman in this category left a telephone solicitation job for a higher paying position at a detox center. Another advanced from fast food crew member to manager. However, even women who had stopped using drugs were impeded from working by physical disabilities and mental health problems—for instance, inability to concentrate due to medications. Despite their mental and physical disabilities, substance-centered women rarely receive public benefits. They must rely on family, partners, or programs for lodging and food.

Dangerous and Unstable Housing Situations. Conviction records and debts for court and supervision fees and treatment create barriers for women looking for housing. Privately owned apartments routinely deny applicants on the basis of past felony convictions. They quickly evict people after new convictions. Further restricting housing options, rules for government-subsidized housing make women with past violent or drug-related offenses ineligible. Public and private housing managers deny housing to women who owe money for past treatment or court- and supervision-related fees. Women who continue to use drugs also contribute to their own housing problems by choosing dangerous or substandard places to live. This combination of restrictive private and subsidized housing policies and poor choices makes stable and safe housing a major issue for women on probation and parole. The housing problem is especially acute for substance-centered women.

Constant movement and substandard housing describe the residential situation of women who continue using drugs. Substance-centered women move repeatedly and stay in places that are unsafe, filthy, and lacking utilities. They stay with people who consume, manufacture, package, and sell drugs. Ruth's housing experience for the twelve months covered in the research illustrates this pattern. In the first month of supervision after release from prison, she moved in with a friend. One week later, she paid $250 a month to rent a room in another woman's apartment. In the third month, Ruth lived in an inexpensive hotel, which she paid for with money borrowed from a man she barely knew. Although she applied for a live-in job taking care of a disabled person, the job did not materialize. As her money was running out, Ruth planned to move in with her mother or borrow money from her for an apartment. In the fourth month, she intended to live with her sister, who would give her "one more chance." Instead, she moved in with her mother and stepfather, both of whom needed care because of illness.

At times, women live in abandoned logging cabins, tents, camping trailers, garages, unused shacks in closed migrant-worker camps, pop-up tents in the woods, or cars. They sleep in bedrooms of friends' children and on their living-room couches. The women may not even know the names of the so-called boyfriends and friends they live with. One woman who camped along the highway always carried a knife as protection against sexual assault.

There are many reasons for repeatedly moving between substandard, dangerous residences. Women move to get away from relatives who engage in illegal activity or are abusive. A relative or partner may keep guns in the house, but conditions of supervision prohibit women from staying in a residence with firearms. Natasha moved out of her boyfriend's place after he abused her. Initially she lived with his mother, then moved to another county to get even farther away. Partners are not the only abusive people women try to escape. Stepparents, parents, children, or siblings also may be abusive. Moving does not always mean safety, because new residences often present their own dangers and drawbacks.

Women also move out of safe living arrangements when family-of-origin members, partners, or roommates refuse to tolerate their continued drug use. One brother told the supervising officer: "This is the last straw. She lied in the past, and I will not tolerate drugs or her former friends in the house." Another relative locked a woman out of the house, after she threatened family members who tried to escort her to outpatient treatment. Relatives told women to leave their homes to protect children from exposure to drug use. Relatives, roommates, and others living with drug-using women become overwrought with worry and anger when women stay in the residence sporadically, fail to contribute to the care or support of children, bring other drug users home, or go off on binges. Relatives and friends find active drug users' lifestyles disruptive, upsetting, and even threatening. They respond by refusing to give the women a place to stay.

In many cases, women chose to leave available, safe homes. Some moved in with partners who were abusive or criminal, especially just after the partners were released from jail or prison. Others gravitated toward drug houses, where other users congregate in a home, apartment, or — in rural areas — collections of cabins, trailers, or tents. Supervising officers prohibited women from staying with criminal intimate partners or at drug houses, but women got around these prohibitions by claiming they lived in approved, safe places that were in reality false addresses.

Although some women stayed at drug houses because they lacked alternatives, most made a conscious choice to live in these settings. Motivations included easy access to drugs as well as evading police and supervising officers. At such properties, residents and visitors behave in ways that invite eviction or expulsion for trespassing. Legitimate renters fail to pay. Drug activity and violence are out in the open. For instance, one woman banged on the on-site apartment manager's door and screamed for help. When he opened the door, she blacked out from alcohol consumption in the apartment hallway. Children are also often unsupervised. Residents and visitors yell at children and physically beat them. All of this activity increases the likelihood of police raids and drug house closures, or eviction of residents and trespassers by property owners. Evictions, police raids, abusive and volatile people, and the low quality of housing contribute to continuing residential instability.

Women who stopped using drugs stayed in relatively more stable and safe places. Danny moved from an old logging camp where she had rented a cabin to subsidized housing. Other women left abusive partners and moved in with relatives, or moved from relatives' homes to their own places. Jen and the female friend who shared her apartment left a third household resident, who urged her to use drugs with him. After she and her friend rented a nicer, larger place, Jen was able to move her children into the house. Often family-of-origin relatives or in-laws help drug-abstaining women with housing. Being drug free enables women to secure live-in positions as caretakers for ill, disabled, or elderly people. Women discover that finding sober roommates and intimate partners to live with is easier when they are drug free. Many can improve their living situations, though they still face some housing barriers due to past convictions and limited incomes. These barriers often result in periods of homelessness or stays in inexpensive motels.

Criminal Social Networks. It is commonplace for substance-centered women to turn to people who use drugs and break other laws for social support. Substance-centered women's criminal networks include parents and grandparents, siblings, intimate partners, teenage and adult children, and friends and associates. Representative examples include grandparents arrested for driving under the influence of intoxicants or domestic violence, and siblings with records for possession, manufacture, and distribution of drugs. Other types of crimes committed by people in support networks include child abuse, sexual assault, murder, forgery, and theft. A typical substance-centered woman gets support from a sister arrested for theft, a friend arrested for drug possession, and then a second friend holding drugs. If they have substance-abstinent and law-abiding relatives, substance-using women usually do not turn to them for social or material support. Instead, they rely on criminal partners, friends, and associates. The high frequency of material and emotional support and companionship coming only from people who break the law distinguishes the substance-centered women from other subgroups.

A few women were pressured by pimps to work as prostitutes, write bad checks, and carry out other illegal activities. However, intimate partners and pimps did not force most women to break the law. In fact, even after the incarceration of their criminal partners, the women usually continued to use drugs and break the law. They turned to other individuals involved in crime and drugs for support. Dependence on alternative criminal elements perpetuates the negative effects of support networks.

For abstinent substance-centered women, support networks were not markedly better. Just a few had networks that were devoid of people with criminal histories. Most networks contained at least some criminally active family or friends. A number of women struggled to leave or avoid abusive or criminally involved partners.

Broken and Troubled Families. Before the research began, most of the women with long histories of crime and substance abuse, who make up the majority of the substance-centered subgroup, had given up their children for adoption or permanently lost custody to a father, a grandparent, or the state. The exceptions were a few first-time offenders who maintained contact and custody. One lived with her teenage son and parents. Another lived in a stable situation with her children and friends, both before and after conviction. More typically, children were dispersed among multiple relatives or a combination of relatives' and foster homes. Children in the custody of relatives — say, a grandparent or an aunt — usually have visits or even live with their mothers along with relatives. Fathers obtain child custody on the basis of the ill effects that women's drug use and other crimes have on the children. Typically if women continue using drugs, fathers with custody will prevent all mother-child contact.

The lifestyle of women on drugs reduces their ability to keep or regain child custody. The courts rarely remove children capriciously. In one case, a woman lost custody of four children after a Child and Family Services Agency worker observed them in her care. The worker noted that she "had lacerations all over her body" and was intoxicated to the point that "she could hardly stand up." Despite repeated warnings over an extended time, many women who continue using drugs miss child-custody hearings and fail to complete required drug treatment. The Child and Family Services Agency then acts to terminate custody.

Children in some contact with their mothers often experience multiple changes in caretakers. Like their mothers, they move repeatedly. Peg's children exemplify this pattern. Her three children (all under age seven) first lived with her mother for a few months. After Peg's mother lost custody, they moved to a foster home, where Peg visited them one hour each week.

In general, children who remain with drug-using mothers are exposed to people engaged in drug use, periods of homelessness, or the same substandard living conditions as their mothers. They have troubles of their own, particularly if they are adolescents. Children's troubles extend to delinquency, truancy, school suspensions for sexual assault, drugs and alcohol use, early sexual activity, running away, and anger. Women therefore struggle to parent their troubled children and meet their special needs.

Women beyond drug use attempt to regain custody of their children, if this is a possibility. Women's abstinence leads to actions by the Child and Family Services Agency and relatives' efforts to help them reunite with children not permanently in the custody of others. Jen, for example, explained she was in a "race" with her "ex" to stay clean and get her five children back. Once women stop using drugs, the courts more often grant visits, then overnight stays, and finally custody. This progression may not occur, though, when women experience resistance from relatives. Irreversible past custody decisions prevent other women from reuniting with their children.

Interconnected Troubles. The numerous problems of substance-centered women grow in relation to each other. This was the case for Shannon. She owed thousands of dollars of restitution after a conviction for failing to declare her husband's income when she applied for state medical insurance. Her financial problems worsened when her husband was laid off at the beginning of her year of supervision. During that year, Shannon's husband left her and then returned. He lost and found jobs. At one point, the couple's financial situation was so bad that they lost their car. When they purchased another car, they could not even pay for gas. Shannon received support from a state agency to care for her parents. When her father died, she lost the part of her already limited income provided by the state for his care. According to mental health care providers, Shannon relapsed into drug use because she was depressed about her father's death and her financial situation. At that point, the police arrested her for possession of a controlled substance. She told the supervising officer that she had no money for food and was ineligible for food stamps, and that "everything is so bad in my life, it feels as if I'm falling apart. I'm at the end of my rope." Financial pressures and the collapse of fragile income sources contributed to her drug relapse.

Suzanne also experienced a combination of interrelated problems that produced severe strains. She attributed her heavy marijuana use to being "mentally twisted" from several years of caring for her severely disabled child. During her year of supervision, new problems arose. She earned less than $400 a month caring for her boyfriend's very ill relative. An injury at a court-ordered community service job prevented her from working. Her disabled daughter was in and out of the hospital. Then Suzanne contracted pneumonia and needed minor surgery for an unrelated illness. She was living with her boyfriend, who began drinking heavily and abusing her. After several weeks, he terminated their relationship by locking her out of the residence without her belongings. State medical insurance had run out, so she could not get the mental health counseling she needed to help her with the numerous pressures she faced.

The histories of women beyond drug use include out-of-home placements during childhood; sexual abuse by a father, stepfather, or cousin; and running away as a child. All of these experiences affected their educational attainment and emotional well-being. Medical and dental problems, disability, lack of a phone or car, and large restitution bills for thousands of dollars added to their troubles. Mental health problems created employment challenges for Tina, whose anxiety disorder made it difficult for her to work as a waitress. In case notes, the supervising officer wrote that Tina's boss told her she was "too nervous" to do her job. In contrast to the boss's negative assessment, the mental health counselor said Tina was "lucky she was able to work that many hours with her ADHD." Women like Tina, who stop using drugs despite damaging backgrounds and continuing problems, still face numerous challenges and stresses in their lives.

Whether or not they still use drugs, substance-centered women are almost always on the margins of the workforce and dependent on resources that periodically run out or have rules locking the women out of the recipient pool. In addition, many women lack transportation. They cannot look for a job, get to work, or get to required treatment and community supervision groups and appointments. They often must contend with partners who are abusive or binge on alcohol or drugs. Added to these problems are mandated hours of community service and fees for supervision. As an illustration of how problems cluster together, one woman was afraid to attend a treatment program she needed because evening travel put her at risk of attack by the people she was scheduled to testify against. Another woman delayed treatment because the program that evaluated her for substance abuse insisted she pay in full before sending out the results required by potential treatment providers. These combined pressures not only create barriers to getting treatment, but can push women to escape into drug use or abscond from supervision.

Interconnected Resources. With very few exceptions, substance-centered women's education is limited, and they are unable to obtain and hold steady jobs with decent pay. Lucy, convicted of using stolen prescription pads to illegally obtain pain medication, is one exception. She stands out from other women because she had attained a fairly high level of education in the medical field. She was already in college when she first used drugs, so she did not experience their usual devastating impact on educational achievement and related job opportunities. She was one of the few women who attained even modest means. During the year of supervision,

Lucy received a promotion and a raise at her full-time job. Despite a brief term in jail, Lucy kept her children from learning about her conviction. While she was in jail, the children remained at home with her husband. After release, Lucy joined them again in their stable and safe residence.

The Violent Surroundings of Violence-Involved Women

Women with violence-dominated crime usually do not face the multitude of serious problems that substance-centered women do. They have more education and consistent income sources. A few had finished the tenth or eleventh grade; several had completed a high-school education or received a GED; and one finished some college courses while incarcerated. Several received food stamps, and some received welfare support. Husbands brought in part or all of the family income. Most of those who worked had stable, though low-paying jobs — for example, as a delicatessen manager. Eleven of the thirteen women consistently lived in safe places, either with a parent, in subsidized housing, with friends, or, in one case, in a group home for the mentally ill.

Although a few violence-involved women ran away as juveniles and lived in juvenile group homes or institutions, they typically lacked prior adult criminal convictions. If they had a criminal history, it was restricted to violence. Also, unlike the substance-centered women, only a few of the violence-involved women had any mental illness. A few who mentioned diagnoses like depression, anxiety, repressed anger, and bipolar disorder did receive therapy and medication. In many respects, the violence-involved women enjoyed more stable living situations and fewer difficulties than the substance-centered women.

What sets the violence-involved women apart from others is their high degree of enmeshment in networks populated by violent and abusive people. They consistently have histories marked by extreme trauma from violence and family disruption. They are very similar to a group of ten women in a sample of forty that Daly (1994; also see Simpson, Yahner, and Dugan 2009) identified in another study of offenders. Daly called the women "harmed-and-harming" (26). The finding that violent women were often previously harmed by violence applies to the women in my study as well.

Two examples show how violence and trauma permeate the lives of violence-involved women. Elissa's father, who sexually abused her and several other children in the family, had recently committed suicide. Her mother was serving a multiyear term for acting as an accomplice to her husband's crimes of child abuse. Anna, another violence-involved woman, described frequent whippings from her father as a child. When she was a teenager, her father forced her to put her baby up for adoption. Later, she married and then divorced a sexually abusive man. She attributed her stabbing of her second husband and several neighbors to her "rage" over the abuse she had endured over the years. She subsequently left her second husband because he was "cruel," "controlling," and "alcoholic." Despite the separation, the abuse continued into the year of supervision. Her second husband raped her when she stopped by his place to visit. More than any other subgroup, for violence-involved women, trauma and abuse occurred repeatedly at different points over their lives, including the research year.

The Dependence of Partner-Influenced Women

Partner-influenced women range in education from below high school to completion of some college courses. They were either unemployed or earned limited income from part-time or temporary work. The partner-influenced woman with the highest income earned just $1,070 a month. Drug and alcohol use and mental illness did not play any part in partner-influenced women's illegal acts. Only one partner-influenced woman, Kimberly, had committed multiple prior offenses. She had assisted different men, lying to police about one's whereabouts and driving the get-away car for another, who had committed a robbery.

Like many substance-centered women, partner-influenced women rely on very abusive partners for material or emotional help and companionship. For example, to protect her partner from having his probation revoked, Sally switched from the passenger's seat to the driver's in order to take the rap for trying to elude a police officer during a chase. This partner regularly beat Sally during the year. Kimberly described her partner's most serious abuse as twisting her arm and dragging her from room to room. Lack of options often prevents women from leaving abusive partners. For instance, Kimberly could not leave her partner and live with her brother, who was on federal probation for bank robbery, because supervision requirements prohibited living with a felon. Three of the six partner-influenced women left abusive partners, but one of those began seeing another man who beat her.

The Relative Advantages of Economic Offenders

Compared to the women described so far, economic offenders are better off. They do not have the deeply rooted, long-standing troubles that characterize other subgroups. But better off does not mean well off. Like the white-collar women offenders Daly (1989) studied two decades ago, none of the women in my study stole from the workplace while in high-level jobs. They had low-level management or service jobs. Although some described problems with domestic violence, when compared with substance-centered, violence-involved, and partner-influenced women, these women had more access to noncriminal support networks, legitimate work, and public benefits programs like welfare and unemployment insurance. Additionally, the negative health and lifestyle consequences of continued drug and alcohol use and persistent mental illness do not intensify the problems of economic offenders.

One-time economic offenders and repeat economic offenders differ from each other in the stability and adequacy of their housing. The majority of one-time offenders lived in stable, safe places with nonabusive partners, parents, friends, children, and adult offspring. In contrast, several repeat economic offenders lived in places that supported their illegal activity, or had to move because of their illegal activity or inadequate resources. One repeat economic offender, Cheri, told the supervising officer that she moved to her husband's place to leave her alcoholic boyfriend. Later she moved back with her boyfriend, because her husband had crack in the home. Another repeat economic offender, Michelle, who was addicted to gambling, moved to Nevada, where gambling is legal. Faced with the only option of living in a work release center, one woman absconded to another state, where she committed a new offense. Then, released from jail, she moved to a new apartment in the county where she was under supervision. After being evicted from the new apartment, she absconded again. Committing repeated economic offenses is associated with untenable living situations, which may result from the refusal of family members to provide housing due to recurring illegal behavior, or from the multiple problems aside from criminal involvement that these women face.

In contrast to repeat economic offenders, almost all one-time economic offenders had finished high school. Many had attended or graduated from two- or four-year colleges. During the study year, one worked on a master's degree, and two others were in bachelors' programs, in pharmacy and education. Only one had dropped out of school as early as the eighth grade. Repeat economic offenders are more heterogeneous in their education, divided about equally among three levels: less than high school, a high-school degree, and some college. Thus, many lacked the educational advantages shared by the one-time economic offenders.

One-time economic offenders usually held middle-class jobs, like billing clerk or preschool teacher, or lower-paying but steady jobs, like house or hotel cleaners. When circumstances change and they are under pressure, they adapt and remain employed. One typical woman in this subgroup switched from job to job, but she worked most of the year. When her employer refused to give her time off from waitressing to attend the "theft talk," Saturday "work crews," and the "penitentiary tour" that were conditions of her supervision, she took a new job counseling families at a funeral home. Despite a criminal record, a work history gives women access to unemployment benefits, workers' compensation, and opportunities for securing new employment. Some one-time economic offenders chose not to work in order to stay home with children or to take maternity leave. Some husbands supported women who did not work. These women had the choice not to work and did not face the barriers to finding and keeping a job that so often affected other subgroups. Though not all one-time economic offenders were advantaged in the workforce or through the economic contributions of a partner, they did not suffer the most extreme situations of no work history and little or no legitimate income.

Few economic offenders mentioned mental health problems or treatment to interviewers. When they did, it was apparent that participation in the workforce, stable living situations, and employed partners or parents led to greater access to private mental health care. For example, one supervising officer wrote that a woman's depression and related eating disorder had caused her to cash two stolen checks. The officer noted that after receiving help from eating disorder counselors, physicians, and a nutritionist, the woman resumed an active, law-abiding lifestyle. Similarly, even though another woman was arrested for two thefts during supervision, a psychiatric assessment indicated no need for treatment; this served as the basis for early termination of supervision. Access to a private mental health assessment and care enabled lawyers for employed economic offenders to present illegal activity as part of a resolved, temporary mental health problem. Unlike substance-centered women, who rarely leave mental health problems behind them, economic offenders often recover from periods of depression or other mental illnesses.

Intimate partners contributed to the lawbreaking of a few one-time economic offenders. Sarah told the supervising officer that she collected unemployment fraudulently after her husband took their assets and left her with debts. Another woman forged a check to avoid "setting off" her husband's "drinking spells." She anticipated an alcohol binge if he found out they were short of money to buy electronic equipment he wanted. Women also fraudulently obtained public benefits (e.g., food stamps) through cooperation or complicity with partners. Despite the negative influences of a few partners, economic offenders usually had several friends, family, or children with no prior or present involvement in illegal activity. During the year, some added therapists, clergy, or treatment program staff to their essentially noncriminal support networks.

Although they had noncriminal support, a subset of repeat economic offenders depended on people who joined with them in committing economic crimes. One woman belonged to a gang that received and sold stolen goods. Another worked with her husband to promote prostitution at an adult sex shop. A third said that she and her partner "wrote checks for stuff they wanted." Even if they coordinated with others to break the law, the economic offenders were not enmeshed in the predominantly criminal networks that characterized the substance-centered women. Because their lifestyles do not have the negative impact found for substance-centered women, noncriminal people may accept and support economic offenders, despite their lawbreaking and some criminal associates.

Life in the Middle Class: Marijuana Cultivators

Middle-class women make up the group of marijuana cultivators. Most had completed some college courses; the least educated was a woman who had earned only a GED. The woman with the lowest paying, least stable job operated a failing cleaning business with her husband. Another lived on disability payments, earnings from odd jobs, and her husband's social security. More-successful women had fair or good salaries of their own and additional income from their husbands. For example, one woman had a combined income with her husband of over $3,800 a month.

Several elements in their histories reflect marijuana cultivators' middle-class status. The women lived with partners or, in a few cases, children who knew about or helped grow marijuana. These associates, however, had not committed other illegal acts. Like the economic offenders, the marijuana cultivators did not have the highly criminal networks of substance-centered women, or the very violent networks of violence-involved women. Even the marijuana cultivators who relied on one or more people with prior drug convictions also drew support from others without drug and crime involvement.

Compared with other women, those who cultivated marijuana had more stable lives. They lived with their children, held jobs, or had other legitimate income sources. Several were treated for anxiety or depression, but none mentioned more severe forms of mental illness. Notably, the one woman with new arrests during the year remained in the community. None absconded or ended the year incarcerated. Their resources, limited prior contact with the justice system, and predominantly law-abiding support networks put marijuana cultivators in a good position to get help and to address any difficulties in their lives.

Child Maltreatment: Limited Resources, Limited Criminality

Women under supervision solely because of child maltreatment had very minimal resources. Most had failed to complete high school, though three were working on GEDs. One had finished high school, and one had completed some college. Some had no income. Others lived on their husbands' relatively low wages (under $2,000 a month) or low-paying, temporary jobs. One woman received welfare support, and a few had food stamps.

Most women in the child maltreatment subgroup said they had never used any illegal drugs and reported no involvement with the mental health system. These women did not have an identifiable characteristic support network. At one extreme, one woman had nobody to call on for material or emotional help. At the other extreme, a few women had large, noncriminal networks consisting of parents, siblings, and other relatives.

In this small subgroup, women had unique difficulties. Marlee's partner, the father of one of her children, threatened and physically beat their daughter as well as Marlee. Although Marlee left him, she maintained contact because she needed his financial support and because "he is the child's father." Unable to find better places, a few women lived in substandard housing that contributed to charges of child neglect. Women's poverty and dependence contributed to their neglect of their children or exposing them to danger.

At the beginning of the year, at least some of each woman's children lived with relatives or in foster care. With little or no other illegal activity and no drug use, the women worked successfully with the Child and Family Services Agency toward increased contact and eventual reunification with their children.

RACE AND ETHNICITY, DOMINANT ILLEGAL
ACTIVITY, AND RELATIVE DISADVANTAGE

Race and ethnicity affect a person's standing in a society. U.S. statistics reveal that Native Americans, African Americans, and certain subgroups of Hispanics are overrepresented in jails and prisons, and on probation and parole (Glaze and Bonczar 2007; U.S. Department of Justice 2008). In the general population, these groups also are disadvantaged in education and earnings, as well as on numerous quality of life measures, including health (Proctor and Dalaker 2003). Race-based discrimination segregates African Americans especially in communities marked by extreme disadvantage (Krivo et al. 1998; Krivo and Peterson 2000). Consistent with national statistics, the introduction to this book provided evidence of African and Native American women's overrepresentation in community supervision caseloads in the two research counties. This section considers whether some racial and ethnic groups in the two counties differ in their dominant illegal activities, or in their disadvantages and troubles.

Race and ethnicity are connected to the types of crimes women commit (see tables 3.1 and 3.2). Especially for Native American women, but also for white women, the majority are in contact with the courts because of drug use. The comparison of Hispanic and non-Hispanic women shows that in both groups, the most common dominant crime is drug use, with just over 40 percent of Hispanic women and just over 60 percent of non-Hispanic women involved with the courts for this reason. The small numbers of minority women and the few women in some illegal activity subgroups make other comparisons tentative. A few things stand out, though. All three Asian women committed only economic offenses. Only white women grew marijuana. Compared to other women, Hispanics were less often substance-centered and more often violence-involved. All of these differences are small. Although they reflect the characteristics of women considered in the study, they are not generalizable to larger populations.

TABLE 3.1. *Dominant crime subgroups of women in the study, by race and ethnicity*

		Percent (and number) by race/ethnicity			
Dominant crime	Asian (N = 3)	Black/ African American (N = 16)	Native American (N = 22)	White (N = 328)	total (N = 369)
Substance-centered	0.0	43.8 (7)	81.8 (18)	61.9 (203)	61.8 (228)
Economic only	100.0 (3)	25.0 (4)	4.5 (1)	16.8 (55)	17.1 (63)
Violence-involved	0.0	12.5 (2)	9.1 (2)	2.7 (9)	3.5 (13)
Marijuana cultivation	0.0	0.0	0.0	3.7 (12)	3.3 (12)
Child maltreatment	0.0	0.0	0.0	2.7 (9)	2.4 (9)
Partner-influenced	0.0	0.0	4.5 (1)	1.5 (5)	1.6 (6)
Drug manufacture and trade	0.0	0.0	0.0	0.9 (3)	0.8 (3)
Died during study	0.0	6.3 (1)	0.0	0.6 (2)	0.8 (3)
Driving or unclear	0.0	12.5 (2)	0.0	9.1 (30)	8.7 (32)

I analyzed the data to show whether the racial and ethnic groups had similar proportions on probation and parole. Only the substance-centered subgroup and the economic offender subgroup contained enough women of different races and ethnicities to make the comparisons. First I compared African American, Native American, and white women. Then I compared Hispanic and non-Hispanic women. I made the comparisons separately for the women whose dominant illegal activity involved drugs or economic offenses. I did this to show whether, for women with similar dominant illegal activities, there were racial or ethnic differences in the proportions on parole as opposed to probation.

When just the substance-centered women are considered, quite similar proportions of the three largest racial groups were on parole rather than probation. Of seven substance-centered African American women, 14.3 percent (one) was on parole. Of the eighteen Native Americans, 22.2 percent (four) were on parole. Of 203 white substance-centered women, 20.2 percent (41) were on parole. Also, for substance-centered women, the

TABLE 3.2. *Dominant crime subgroups of women in the study, by identification as Hispanic*

	Percent (and number) by identification as Hispanic		
Dominant crime	Hispanic (N = 37)	not Hispanic (N = 332)	total (N = 369)
Substance-centered	43.2 (16)	63.9 (212)	61.8 (228)
Economic only	21.6 (8)	16.6 (55)	17.1 (63)
Violence-involved	10.8 (4)	2.7 (9)	3.5 (13)
Marijuana cultivation	0.0	3.6 (12)	3.3 (12)
Child maltreatment	2.7 (1)	2.4 (8)	2.4 (9)
Partner-influenced	2.7 (1)	1.5 (5)	1.6 (6)
Drug manufacture and trade	5.4 (2)	0.3 (1)	0.8 (3)
Died during study	0.0	0.9 (3)	0.8 (3)
Driving or unclear	13.5 (5)	8.1 (27)	8.7 (32)

proportions on parole are very similar for Hispanics (18.8 percent, or three of sixteen substance-centered women) and non-Hispanics (20.3 percent, or 43 of 212 substance centered women). No African American or Native American women with economic-only illegal activity, and just 9.1 percent (five of fifty-five) of white economic offenders were on parole. Similarly small proportions of Hispanic (12.5 percent, or one of eight) and non-Hispanic (7.2 percent, or four of fifty-five) economic offenders were on parole. Thus, for the two largest illegal activity subgroups (substance-centered and economic), similar proportions of African American, Native American, white, and Hispanic women were on parole rather than probation. Any effects of the incarceration that precede parole are about evenly distributed over the racial and ethnic groups. Also, regardless of race and ethnicity, a sizable majority of the women in the study were on probation.

I also looked for connections between women's disadvantages and their race and identification as Hispanic (see tables 3.3 and 3.4). Examples of disadvantages include having a criminal intimate partner, illness, and unemployment. Using the computer software for qualitative data analysis, I identified and coded the different disadvantages that could affect women's quality of life and criminality by reading the 369 qualitative cases. I made

TABLE 3.3. *Disadvantages of substance-centered women in the study, by race and ethnicity*

	Percent (and number) by race/ethnicity		
Disadvantages	African American (N = 7)	Native American (N = 18)	White (N = 203)
Unstable/unsafe residence	57.1 (4)	55.6 (10)	70.0 (142)
No work	42.9 (3)	22.2 (4)	6.4 (13)
Criminal family of origin	42.9 (3)	61.1 (11)	33.9 (69)
Criminal friends	71.4 (5)	66.7 (12)	41.4 (84)
Criminal partner	42.9 (3)	55.6 (10)	49.8 (101)
Current domestic violence	57.1 (4)	22.2 (4)	36.9 (75)
Gang involvement	14.3 (1)	5.6 (1)	1.5 (3)

the racial and ethnic comparisons of disadvantages only for substance-centered women, because so few racial and ethnic minorities had other dominant offenses. Parallel to the process for examining racial and ethnic differences in parole, I first compared African American, Native American, and white women. Then I compared Hispanic and non-Hispanic women. I found subtle rather than extreme differences between the groups.

The most pronounced difference for substance-centered women is that African American and Native Americans are most likely to have three particular disadvantages. First, African American and Native American women's support networks tend to contain at least some criminal people. Second, the African American women tend to be victimized by intimate partner violence during the study year. Third, African Americans more often experience unemployment throughout the entire year of supervision. Compared to Hispanic women, non-Hispanics more often have a partner involved in illegal activity. Very few women in any racial or ethnic group belonged to gangs. The groups also differ minimally, if at all, in the stability and safety of place of residence and in involvement with criminal intimate partners. The experiences and processes leading to probation and parole seem to have a leveling effect, so women of different racial and ethnic groups are fairly homogeneous in their problems once they are under community supervision.

TABLE 3.4. *Disadvantages of substance-centered women in the study, by identification as Hispanic*

Disadvantages	Percent (and number) by identification as Hispanic	
	Hispanic (N = 16)	Not Hispanic (N = 212)
Unstable/unsafe residence	62.5 (10)	68.9 (146)
No work	0.0	9.4 (20)
Criminal family of origin	50.0 (8)	35.4 (75)
Criminal friends	43.8 (7)	46.7 (99)
Criminal partner	43.8 (7)	50.4 (107)
Current domestic violence	31.2 (5)	36.8 (78)
Gang involvement	6.3 (1)	14.6 (31)

Several disadvantages coded in the qualitative data occur rarely, for ten or fewer women. Though rare, they pose serious challenges for individual women. Such problems include severe illness or chronic pain, disability, lack of transportation or phone, illegal work, dependence on an abusive or criminal intimate partner, partner's drug addiction or alcoholism, suicidal or violent behavior during the year, subsistence on food stamps, lack of medical insurance, and very large debts, typically for restitution. For the substance-centered women, these less common disadvantages also occur in about the same proportions for all racial and ethnic groups.

The Native American women stand out from others in the high proportion (44.4 percent, or eight of eighteen) with prior or current access to special programs in their community. The resources available to Native Americans include tribal-sponsored substance abuse treatment, housing, counseling, and job training and placement. African American and Hispanic women lack parallel access to special programs focused on their ethnic or racial group. Later chapters show how such availability of resources affects community supervision experiences and outcomes.

Residential segregation and community disadvantage can explain why more African American and Native American than white women lack employment during the year. These structural problems also can explain why African Americans and Native Americans more often had intimate partners and friends with arrest records. Furthermore, racial and ethnic group differences may account for the choice of and opportunity for illegal activities or prior police or court decisions that move some women deeper into the justice system than others. However, once on probation or parole, the racial and ethnic groups in the study have fairly similar profiles. The exceptions are that, at the study site, Native American women enjoy access to some special resources, and African Americans experience more disadvantages related to work and support networks.

AGE AND DOMINANT CRIMINAL ACTIVITY

I found some age differences between women in the six major illegal activity subgroups (see table 3.5). Fewer than 20 percent of substance-centered women were under twenty-five years old, but about half of partner-influenced and violence-involved women were in that youngest age category. Substance-centered women tended to be between twenty-five and thirty-four, and quite a few were thirty-five and older. The older age of many substance-centered women results from their long histories of drug use and related involvement in the justice system. Most marijuana cultivators were over thirty-four, suggesting that this offense was heavily influenced by the women's birth cohort. For the substance-centered women, age did not differentiate who failed, who managed in the community despite drug use, and who avoided drug use for the entire study year. For the sample as a whole, the largest group of women was between twenty-five and thirty-four (41.2 percent), the second largest group was thirty-five and older (36.7 percent), and the smallest group was under twenty-five (22.1 percent).

These statistics on age ground women at a point in their lives. They help us anticipate what the women are up against as they try to stay out of prison or jail, and improve their quality of life. Substance-centered women are older, and as noted, for most of them, drug use and justice system involvement go back for many years. Therefore, the burdens of medical, social, family, and other problems caused by substance use and prior incarcerations fall on them. The younger women in the partner-influenced and violence-involved subgroups might be particularly amenable to programming that stresses continued education and coaching in life skills necessary for a successful adulthood. Some of their offenses, like firebombing a person or fighting with peers, strike me as driven by youthful impulsive-

TABLE 3.5. *Dominant crime subgroups of women in the study, by age*

	Percent (and number) in subgroups by age					
Age	substance-centered (N = 227)	economic only (N = 63)	violence-involved (N = 13)	marijuana cultivation (N = 12)	child maltreatment (N = 9)	partner-influenced (N = 6)
Under 25	18.5 (42)	30.2 (19)	46.2 (6)	0.0	33.3 (3)	50.3 (3)
25–34	46.3 (105)	30.2 (19)	15.4 (2)	33.3 (4)	55.6 (5)	16.7 (1)
35+	35.2 (80)	39.7 (25)	38.5 (5)	66.7 (8)	11.1 (1)	33.3 (2)

Note: Age was missing for one woman. This table does not include data for 38 women in other subgroups, or for whom a subgroup could not be determined.

ness. Other offenses grow out of their own victimization. Community supervision needs to support their transition to adulthood and address the trauma of victimization. Several in the oldest group of marijuana cultivators are motivated by the drug's capacity to ease the physical pain associated with deteriorating health and aging. Effective community interventions must respond to women's histories and place in the life course.

CONCLUSION

Especially for substance-centered and violence-involved women, troubles are interconnected and clustered together. Singular, disconnected problems characterize women whose crimes are restricted to economic gain, marijuana cultivation, or child maltreatment. Crises do affect this second group. However, these women typically do not face a series of escalating problems that have extended over years. Women with different patterns of illegal activity are distinct from each other on numerous crucial dimensions and cannot meaningfully be studied as a homogeneous group.

The substance-centered subgroup that constitutes two-thirds of women under supervision has the most deeply rooted troubles. They also present with crisis situations related to housing, support networks containing people with substance abuse problems or criminal histories, abusive partners, and children who are dispersed, troubled, or both. Moving from place to place and living in unsavory places make substance-centered women especially difficult to supervise. Supervising officers cannot find them, and their problems increase due to exposure to persistent negative influences and dangerous living conditions. Also, many women carry negative emotions after permanently losing child custody and contact. Others expend their energies trying to regain their parental roles. Part 2 of this book considers whether and how supervising officers respond to women's varying and often complex histories and immediate needs and crises. It also considers differences in county responses, and the results of alternative approaches.

II

OUTCOMES IN THE TWO COUNTIES

4

Drug Users Who Fail

You can just run through this system — no problem. They
have too many people to shuffle through. You just fill out paper
and no changes in personality or behavior is made.
APRIL, Traditional County

A simple comparison shows very little difference between Traditional and Gender Responsive Counties in the proportions of substance-centered women who failed during the year. In Traditional County, 46.2 percent (61 of 132) failed, and 42.2 percent (46 of 109) failed in Gender Responsive County. The small size of this difference means it may be due to chance. In addition, it is possible that incarceration by the end of the year resulted more from the higher level of supervision in Gender Responsive County than from women's actual behavior. As a result, the Gender Responsive County failure rate may be exaggerated. In this chapter, I use extensive qualitative data to develop a valid comparison of the supervision experiences of substance-centered women who ended the year absconded, incarcerated, or with new offenses in the two counties. I first demonstrate the effects of different tactics, and then I show how two other types of influence shape outcomes. One type is personal choices; the other is service and program inadequacies, aside from supervision.

LIMITED AND NARROW SUPERVISION
IN TRADITIONAL COUNTY

Officers delivered limited and narrow supervision to just one of the failing substance-centered women in Gender Responsive County, but to nineteen of them in Traditional County. In Traditional County, supervising officers gathered little information from employment counselors or treatment providers. Instead of adopting the gender-responsive ideals of wraparound services and a continuum of care, Traditional County's officers tended to focus narrowly on one facet of a woman's character or circumstances.

Supervision at a limited level was not justified by women's having only limited needs. For example, in Traditional County, Peg contended with numerous interconnected troubles. As noted earlier, she broke the law to avoid beatings by her abusive partner, she had an unstable living situation (first with her mother, then with her partner, and then in a van until it was repossessed), and she lost child custody during the year. The very few failing substance-centered women who worked legally did so sporadically, holding low-paying jobs like selling jewelry at an outdoor market or doing seasonal landscaping, baby-sitting, temporary clerical work, and telemarketing. Prior incarcerations and lengthy records were the norm. All but one woman had been convicted previously. Mental illness included bipolar and anxiety disorders. Women receiving limited, narrow supervision often had previously attempted suicide. Several used multiple drugs before or during their teen years. Their histories commonly included participation in one or more treatment programs. Based on drug history, mental illness, domestic violence, employment history, or prior record, the women on limited supervision in Traditional County would have received more intense supervision in Gender Responsive County.

Limited and narrow supervision practices that were linked to failure for the substance-centered group included the practice of chronicling problems but taking no action to address them, breaks in services, gaps in substance-abuse intervention, and mismatching women's problems with supervising officers' interventions.

Chronicling Women's Troubles

Case notes about Chris illustrate Traditional County's chronicling practices. The supervising officer described Chris's many interconnected troubles in case notes, but he focused narrowly on an incident in which she drank alcohol, and on his subsequent efforts to prove and correct her "criminal thinking." Case notes indicate that Chris felt overwhelmed after she ran into a man who had abused her daughter. The supervising officer wrote: "We talked about the right and wrong ways to deal with situations." Two weeks later, the notes read:

Distressed because of problems at work. Other employees treated her like she had the plague. Friend she lives with is not a healthy person to be around. Fifty dollars behind in the rent because of missing work from the car wreck.

Three weeks after that, the officer noted:

Laid off three days a week. A money order was taken from her house. It was her rent. Going to physical therapy because of car accident. Daughter to arrive from another state.

After two more weeks, Chris admitted using alcohol, and the supervising officer wrote: "Talked about criminal thinking. I scheduled a polygraph." A week later, the officer documented talking with Chris about the polygrapher's conclusion that she had lied about the money. The officer told Chris she was in relapse, and ordered her to participate more days each week in her substance abuse treatment program. He also directed her to meet with him every week. He did not refer her to the state employment office for help finding a different job, or talk with her about finding new housing, what happened to the money, or her medical problems. The officer focused on detecting lies, correcting "criminal thinking," and referring Chris again to the substance abuse program she was already attending. The supervision tactics did not provide access to new resources, but instead concentrated on the officer's own efforts to alter Chris's "criminal thinking."

Given that a focus on changing criminal thinking differentiated the counties, it is worth considering what this approach entails. Efforts to change offenders' criminal thinking derive from cognitive-behavior therapy, a well-defined psychological treatment. Based on the assumption that offenders learned to think in deficient and distorting ways, "programs for offenders . . . emphasize individual accountability and attempt to teach offenders to understand the thinking processes and choices that immediately preceded their criminal behavior" (Lipsey, Landenberger, and Wilson 2007, 4). Considerable empirical research shows that the approach is most effective when it incorporates anger control and interpersonal problem solving skills, when treatment is carefully implemented, and when practitioners are well trained (ibid., 22–23). Traditional County supervising officers tried to influence behavior by changing criminal thinking, but they certainly did not carefully implement a program of therapy through a series of counseling sessions. At times, supervising officers focused only on criminal thinking. This can decontextualize the situation and produce a mismatch between what happens in the women's lives and minds, and what supervising officers say and do. Although research confirms the effectiveness of well-implemented cognitive-behavior therapy as a part of correctional programming, the realities of the way Traditional County officers implemented the therapy explain its apparent ineffectiveness with the women in this study.

Another feature of Traditional County supervision, the practice of chronicling, completely separates women's troubles from supervising officers' judgments about compliance with supervision. The officer describes a woman's problems in case notes, but acts only in response to whether or not she meets supervision requirements. Chronicling signals that compliance is the real point of supervision. Women's difficulties, such as domestic violence or joblessness, are like noise that is observed and noted. Stacey is an example of someone who received limited intervention despite chronicling of multiple troubles. Stacey's children were placed in foster care before the year began, so she lost access to subsidized housing for parents and children. Just before she lost her housing, the supervising officer did a home visit and noted there were "no problems." After a new conviction, the officer made several notes about Stacey, indicating that a work program deemed her unemployable; she saw a counselor at the Community Mental Health Agency for drug counseling and treatment of bipolar disorder; and she regained child custody, continued to use methamphetamines, and again lost child custody and housing. The supervising officer told Stacey to return to the outpatient treatment program she had previously attended. The officer also periodically sanctioned her with spending days in jail. Though the officer recorded Stacey's difficulties in the case notes, his responses to those problems were minimal in comparison to their gravity.

Often Traditional County supervising officers described continuing drug use and other criminal behaviors over weeks or months, yet at the same time the officers had limited contact with the women and made no interventions aside from warnings. Then, at a tipping point, officers noted sanctions like a few days to several weeks in jail or the work release center, or a revocation. Gina's supervision is an example of the tipping point dynamic. The police charged Gina, a continuing methamphetamine user, with a new instance of possessing a controlled substance very soon after supervision began. The supervising officer noted that Gina called to say she could not keep an appointment because she was "in detox," and that the "detox program would decide what she needed after that." After a few months, the officer wrote that an outpatient program had suspended Gina for continued use of methamphetamines. Gina told the supervising officer that problems with visiting her children tempted her to use drugs. On the research survey form, the supervising officer checked off "help" and "refer" for the problem of substance abuse. The officer checked off "help" for educational needs. The officer did not report helping or making a referral for child visitation issues. He left the choice of substance abuse treatment up to Gina and the staff at the detox center. Other Traditional County officers noted that women they supervised failed to obtain substance abuse evaluations, did not follow through and obtain treatment, and moved from program to program. At some tipping point, the officers sanctioned women or returned them to court for revocation, but even with considerable evidence of drug use, this did not always happen.

Gaps in Services

Particularly in Traditional County, even relatively intensive supervision had gaps in continuity or in the range of interventions. Rita moved from another state where her supervision had stipulated high-level monitoring. Following her suicide attempt early in the year, her supervising officer referred her to the Community Mental Health Agency outreach worker. After that, case notes give monthly updates on office visits, housing arrangements, mental health treatment, and Rita's high-risk pregnancy. When Rita moved in with her mother, the supervising officer transferred her case to another worker who handled that zip code area. Authorities in the other state rejected the new supervising officer's efforts to discharge her early. In the twelfth month of supervision, the new officer transferred Rita to the limited supervision caseload. The supervision level started out high, especially after the suicide attempt. However, limited referrals, the practice of changing supervising officers based on zip code areas, and the goal of reducing supervision to a very low level over the year had the effect of ending Rita's relationship with the first supervising officer and then fragmenting attention to her multiple needs.

Rita is not the only woman in Traditional County whose needs were not met. When Leslie continued breaking the law, she spent time in jail, where a counselor referred her to an outpatient treatment program for substance abuse for sessions four times a week. The supervising officer met with Leslie several times during the year, but did not require substance abuse treatment before or after the referral made by the counselor. Leslie described the benefits of the outpatient substance abuse program:

It's given me a center, a place to start my life over again. I like how it's confidential. The people are warm and sincere.

She also had some criticisms:

There is a time limit to how long you can be in the program — people are graduating that don't seem ready, and the support is completely over once you leave. They [the staff] say that certain things will be worked on but the staff don't follow through. [The program needed] more structure, no tolerance for being late, [and there was] cross talk and people showing up late and nobody seems to care.

Leslie's supervising officer noted the programs she attended, but treatment seemed unconnected to supervision. Leslie felt that aftercare to provide transition services following an intense program was poorly organized and not long enough. Feminist advocates for gender-responsive corrections would argue that the program and Leslie's broader experience with supervision failed to provide a continuum of care.

Weigh the imminent withdrawal of program support for Leslie against elements of her background and situation: multiple drug use starting at age ten, ten years of "shooting up heroin," numerous prior attempts at treatment, a diagnosis as bipolar and a history of depression and suicide, no work history except in prostitution, no teeth, no place to live, and a support network populated exclusively by people who had been arrested for drug-related offenses or assault. Leslie knew that attending a program with little structure and follow-through four times a week for a limited time was not enough to keep her from using drugs and breaking the law again. During the year-end interview, she said she supported herself dealing drugs and working as a prostitute.

Breaking the Chain in Intervention

In Gender Responsive County, a common chain of events pushes women who keep using drugs into increasingly intense substance abuse treatment. The chain starts with detection through drug testing or during frequent office and home visits. It includes substance abuse evaluation and recommended placements, relapses, and then new evaluations and placements. Many Traditional County women with limited and narrow supervision had long histories of using drugs and used drugs extensively during the study year. Yet they were often not tested for drug use or required to undergo substance abuse evaluations. Supervising officers only sporadically linked substance abuse evaluation results to getting women into particular recommended services and programs. When women relapsed, officers did not require progressively intense and secure treatment. The chain from detection of drug use to final placement might be broken at any link.

No drug use testing, no substance abuse treatment. Charlotte told her supervising officer that she had used "meth and heroin for seventeen years." Despite her extensive history of use, drug testing was not required for her. In regard to a seemingly critical area — referral for substance abuse treatment — Charlotte and the supervising officer completed parallel survey forms indicating that the officer did not make any treatment referrals. On the survey forms, the officer checked that he directly helped Charlotte with substance abuse problems, but Charlotte did not check that he had done so.

No assistance in accessing a substance abuse program. Brandi told the interviewer that after police arrested her during the year, the supervising officer "just yelled at me." She also said that the officer told her to attend substance abuse treatment, but ultimately her insurance company actually helped her locate a helpful program.

No evaluation, attending a program that was not recommended. Arlene's supervising officer noted that she failed to make contact. Once she did make contact, she informed the officer that instead of attending the inpatient program they had discussed, she had joined a self-help group that met for one hour a week at her church. The supervising officer noted: "She seems to be doing OK and maybe she is avoiding contact with criminal friends." The officer also told Arlene to undergo a substance abuse evaluation, but she missed the appointment.

Referral to nonexistent aftercare treatment. Sharon completed an in-prison substance abuse treatment program. On her release, the staff there referred her to a three-month aftercare program but did not give her the appropriate paperwork. The supervising officer called and found this aftercare was no longer available. The officer then told Sharon to attend the "wait list group" with another program, but she did not show up. The officer noted no further action.

Attending a program other than the one that was recommended. Megan's supervising officer wrote that Megan attended a program other than the one recommended by the substance abuse evaluator. The officer wrote: "After further discussion, I decided to let her stay [at the program that was not recommended]. She's getting lots of one-on-one. Her feeling about the other [recommended] program is that she has a lot of anger and personal childhood issues to deal with but not yet and she feels like the other program will push too hard and she's not ready yet. Out of respect for that I'm going to defer and let her continue as long as she continues to do her program. I will give her space to make those decisions."

Outpatient treatment that does not stop drug use, with no new evaluation or treatment program. When Stacey tested positive for methamphetamine and marijuana use, she agreed to a sanction of a few days in jail, several hours of community service, and a referral to treatment. At one point during the year, the supervising officer wrote that Stacey had told her substance abuse counselor about spending the night using methamphetamines and having sex in a van full of people. Toward the end of the year, Stacey continued attending outpatient treatment and testing positive for drugs.

I found numerous examples of the sort presented above showing a broken chain between substance abuse detection and aftercare treatment in Traditional County. In Gender Responsive County, the chain broke only when women absconded, or refused and avoided evaluation or treatment.

Mismatched Troubles and Interventions

Because a comprehensive, prioritized assessment of women's needs was not the basis for Traditional County interventions, mismatches occurred between what women needed and what their supervising officers required or did. I sometimes found these mismatches in the data startling. Initially, I coded them as oddities, but I later realized that they seemed odd because of the failure to match women's circumstances to appropriate correctional responses. Stacey's case, mentioned above, provides several examples of mismatches. The supervising officer noted that employment specialists had determined that Stacey was unemployable due to a mental illness that interfered with her interactions with people. Asked what program, including supervision, most helped her during the year, Stacey told the interviewer:

It was a little bit helpful that the PO [Probation Officer] was making me go out there and look for work. It gives me incentive that I can or have to. The head PO is really laid back, not about job contacts, but pretty real. He'll write 'fucking off' or 'do job search.'

She went on to say that the supervising officer did not understand her: "I have a hard time dealing with the public. That's what I'm in treatment for, dealing with strangers and anxiety and they make me get fifteen job contacts a week." The job search requirement conflicted with the mental health and employment specialists' evaluations. A recommendation from the substance abuse counselor that Stacey be in residential treatment — to say nothing of the fact that her living situations were dangerous and unstable — was also inconsistent with the supervising officer's inaction in getting her into residential treatment. At year's end, Stacey was unaware of any move in the direction of residential treatment for her. When the interviewer asked what happened after she stopped reporting for supervision, Stacey said: "Nothing. Nothing happened yet. I left a message and have a doctor's excuse."

Data for Maxine exemplifies another Traditional County mismatch. Maxine had completed a substance abuse treatment program years before, but had relapsed. During the year, on her own initiative, Maxine transferred from an outpatient to a residential treatment program. The supervising officer noted that although she was in residential treatment, "the priority needs to be employment to take care of financial obligations." Maxine later left the residential treatment program and could not be located. In these examples, officers emphasized employment for women whose problems centered on addiction. The Traditional County officers' priorities contrast with Gender Responsive County supervision for Fran, discussed in the next chapter. Fran's supervising officer wrote that she told Fran to attend the Intensive Drug Treatment Program not once but twice each week, and "if that means she is unable to keep her job, treatment is a priority." The next chapter presents additional evidence of the priority that Gender Responsive County gives to very specific treatment modalities recommended by substance abuse specialists.

One pattern I coded as a mismatch is a series of case notes about women who do not report and do not comply with supervision requirements, followed by a final comment about shifting to limited or mail-in supervision, or even terminating supervision. A number of Traditional County women and one Gender Responsive County woman shifted to very limited supervision, despite minimal information about their needs and their apparent noncompliance with supervision. For these women, the phrase *little known and little happening* characterizes supervision.

One additional sort of mismatch of interventions and troubles exists in Traditional County. Supervising officers there refer nearly all women—regardless of their criminal history and health problems—to an HIV/AIDS education and awareness program. In the interviews, no woman identified this program as especially helpful.

Women's Criticism of Limited and Narrow Supervision

Peg, whose many problems with intimate partner violence, living arrangements, and child custody have been discussed, gave her view of limited and narrow supervision:

> They deal with the symptoms not the problem. I was treated like I was less than a human. [Supervision could be improved by] addressing individual needs, not with a cookie cutter. Like cattle, they herd you, tag you, just like cattle. [The state Child and Family Services Agency and substance abuse treatment programs] deal with your needs. Here there is no individual needs assessment.

Another Traditional County woman also disliked limited and narrow supervision:

> I've been in here [jail] most of the time and I haven't been in any programs even though I know they're out there. My PO [probation officer] used a dirty UA [urine analysis drug test] against me when at first she said she wasn't going to. Since I've been here, she'd never come to see me. [A change I'd make would be] more access to information on services like transitional housing and all that.

Because Traditional County did not emphasize a continuum of care from referral to increasingly intense substance abuse treatment followed by aftercare, women criticized the limited attention they received in programs.

Alexandra said about outpatient treatment in Traditional County: "There is not enough counselors to have one-on-one attention, [and what is needed is] more process time, more talk about sexual abuse."

In jail in Traditional County during the twelfth month of her supervision, Charlotte observed:

[My PO] had a different idea of what supervision was supposed to be about, and focused on intimidation and punishment, but I wanted to learn new skills. The PO seemed to take pleasure in making supervision a punishment, scaring the participants.

Charlotte further explained that when she had been on probation in another county, "they made me be employed and report for UAs [urine analysis drug tests] weekly." In the other county, the supervising officer "was cool," there was "an attainable goal," and the officer "worked on specific goals." They "make it a better environment with a personality there to help and support." She went on to say that Traditional County has "lots of jail space" and "no idea or need for resocialization." Key in this description of what was missing in Traditional County is the phrase "a personality there to help and support." As I analyzed data for other subgroups of women, I saw more clearly that Gender Responsive County supervising officers, as well as the substance abuse treatment and other personnel to whom they referred women, were "a personality there to help and support." These officers have considerable positive effects on substance-centered women who manage to stay in the community during the year, crime free and even thriving.

The literature on girls in juvenile court highlights the importance of having "a personality there to help and support." Many substance-centered women have juvenile court histories. Girls in the juvenile justice system search for adults to act as proxy family members, to be "someone to talk to" on a continuing basis (Gaarder, Rodriguez, and Zatz 2004, 569; Sherman 2003). Research documents the fact that such girls are disappointed with probation officers and others who pay attention to them only when they break a rule, violate a condition, or make mistakes. They resent professionals who "just kept telling me what to do" but don't help, and threaten to lock them up (Sherman 2003, 7). Schaffner (2006) concludes from her research in multiple states that the resource girls in trouble most often request is someone to listen. Though an adult when she participated in this study, Charlotte also hoped she would find someone to listen and help her in the justice system.

BROAD AND INTENSE SUPERVISION IN GENDER RESPONSIVE COUNTY

For nearly all substance-centered women, Gender Responsive County officers attempted to provide broad and intense supervision. This included one-on-one help, intensified monitoring after violations or relapses, and high-quality relationships between the women and their supervising officers.

Help and Referrals for Multiple Needs

Meredith is one Gender Responsive County woman who, despite being counted as a failure, had a supervising officer who helped her and made referrals in a great variety of problem areas. This was a first conviction for Meredith. Methamphetamine use had destroyed her front teeth. Embarrassed, she hesitated to follow up on a referral for training as a construction specialist—a job with a decent salary and benefits. The supervising officer countered Meredith's reluctance by explaining that the state employment services would pay for dental work. Community supervisors also counteracted the negative influences of her boyfriend, who was on probation and frequently joined her in taking methamphetamines. The two supervising officers orchestrated a meeting with the couple so that Meredith could tell her boyfriend she wanted one year "away from him to pursue her own identity, sobriety, and a relationship with her children." Struggling with bipolar disorder, Meredith preferred individual rather than group counseling. Community Mental Health Agency staff complied with the supervising officer's request to provide individual help. The broad and intense supervision practices in Meredith's case characterize supervision in Gender Responsive County.

Increased Monitoring and Contact

Gender Responsive County supervision also gave Beverley many services and much support. Despite a new arrest, she seemed to be doing well at the end of a year. After a long history of substance abuse, dealing and manufacturing drugs, incarcerations, and supervision, Beverley had experienced positive changes. She attended Alcoholics Anonymous, Narcotics Anonymous, and substance abuse treatment; participated in social activities with Cocaine Anonymous; and stayed away from her abusive partner. She changed her support network to include fewer criminals and drug users. After a long lapse in her work history, she applied for full-time jobs and held part-time jobs, like selling newspaper subscriptions. She told her supervising officer: "I'm giving my old size five clothes to the women's shelter. I never want to be that size again." Despite her efforts to stop using methamphetamines and to reach a healthy weight, Beverley had an episode of drinking alcohol and cough syrup during the year. While under the influence, she had an automobile accident that resulted in new charges. The supervising officer noted this response to the new charges:

> I told her she would be seeing more of me for a while and she needs to get back on track. We are back to detailed reports on how many AA/NA [Alcoholics Anonymous/Narcotics Anonymous] meetings she must attend. Her boyfriend has been using drugs and she does not want to marry him anymore, but she needs his money.

The officer noted that she increased supervision, required self-help meetings, and encouraged Beverley to continue her progress. Gender Responsive County officers address slips such as Beverley's with increased monitoring, interaction, support, and treatment requirements.

Women's Relationships with Supervising Officers

In chapter 3, I described Shannon's interconnected and growing troubles with high restitution, an unemployed husband, and loss of income after the parent she cared for died. Even though she passed bad checks after a relapse, she perceived her relationship with the Gender Responsive County supervising officer as helpful:

> My PO listens to me as a person and not a felon. I developed a trust and friendship. I go back to my PO for emotional and social support during a difficult family time. The PO can understand where I'm coming from; see what I'm going through. She can understand my locked-in situation. She's like the key I've been waiting for. Being open and honest is what's going to protect you more than lying, like what others do. The PO is here

to help you as long as you're honest. I rely on my PO and am beginning to look at other programs to meet my needs.

By the year-end interview, Shannon had added a treatment program staff member to her support network. She viewed the staff member as "very important" to her. Shannon also added the supervising officer to her network. Her slips and sanctions did not preclude improvements.

Failure Explained by Excessive Control and Monitoring

In the introduction, I raised the concern that high levels of supervision in Gender Responsive County could increase technical violations and incarceration. Higher levels of supervision did result in greater detection of violations. However, supervising officers and judges often responded with alternative actions, such as "doing nothing," required stays at the work release center or jail for a few days to several weeks, more contacts and drug tests, increased attendance at self-help groups, and increased or changed requirements for substance abuse treatment.

One-time or minor violations did not inevitably lead to official violations or incarcerations in either county. For instance, after Beverley's relapse on alcohol and cough syrup led to her arrest for driving under the influence, the Gender Responsive County officer required more office visits and treatment meetings.

Women in the two counties followed different pathways to revocation and reincarceration. As I described above, after a prolonged period of limited supervision, Traditional County women generally reached a tipping point, at which the supervising officer filed for a revocation. The limited and narrow supervision seen so often in Traditional County contributed to this scenario by not providing extensive help and referrals aimed at stopping drug use and related crimes.

In Gender Responsive County, officers steered women to increased treatment and required more monitoring if they kept using drugs. Some situations, though, prompted officers to initiate revocation of community supervision. Officers began the revocation process when women repeatedly used dangerous drugs or lived in unstable and dangerous situations. In a few cases, relatives' pleas that the supervising officer "do something" to stop drug use motivated officers to initiate revocation. In Gender Responsive County, then, alarmingly negative and dangerous circumstances more often prompted supervising officers to return women to prison in order to prevent them from harming themselves through drugs or exposure to violence.

Women's Appreciation of Broad and Intense Supervision

The supervision that Katie experienced represents the extreme for officer intervention in Gender Responsive County. No Traditional County woman's supervision comes close in intensity. At the start of supervision, Katie had just left jail. At different points during the year, she could not obtain needed resources. To address the unavailability of a residential program, the Gender Responsive County officer advocated and negotiated on her behalf, and coordinated services to get her a place to live and substance abuse treatment.

Three months after supervision began, the police charged Katie with a hit-and-run driving infraction and prostitution. A month later, they charged her with possession of a controlled substance. She told the interviewer she worked for an abusive pimp who forced her to commit over a hundred acts of prostitution and other crimes in six months. The supervising officer referred Katie to a specialized program for women in the sex trade and to a self-esteem group. After another month, the police confronted Katie for fighting over drugs. The police report described her as "flying higher than a kite," and she was detained in jail. Once Katie was released, the officer located her and, according to case notes, later arranged her entry into a secure substance abuse treatment program. This plan did not materialize because Katie had completed "the wrong paperwork so cannot go." A few days later, Katie was homeless. Residential programs had no openings for two weeks. A substance abuse counselor gave Katie a $40 voucher for a motel room. By the time a residential treatment bed opened up, Katie had relapsed and thus became ineligible to enter the program. After another arrest, she called her supervising officer from jail, saying she wanted to "stay in" until she went to either the work release center or to residential treatment. The officer wrote:

> I referred her to many different programs with no probability of an entry date soon. She was sent to another county's women's treatment program while living at an Oxford House next door. I decided it was better than releasing with no treatment.

Unable to follow the substance abuse specialists' recommendation for residential treatment, the officer did patch together a placement in an out-of-county Oxford House, with outpatient substance abuse treatment nearby.

At nine months, Katie was clean, living at the Oxford House, attending a treatment group three times a week, scheduled to meet with a mental health worker, and receiving grief counseling to address the loss of her child several years earlier. Katie said that being on parole helped her the most, because the supervising officer "knows my needs." She praised the woman-only program she attended for helping with "prostitution issues" and teaching her she could get away from prostitution.

EXCEPTIONS IN TRADITIONAL COUNTY

I do not want to overemphasize distinctions between Traditional and Gender Responsive Counties. Traditional County supervised some women on specialized intensive caseloads. Especially on those caseloads, Traditional County women's experiences are quite similar to those of women under supervision in Gender Responsive County.

Susan, a woman on a Traditional County specialized intensive caseload, is a case in point. She received a high level of oversight and contact, and a wide range of services. The supervising officer regularly coordinated with staff at a series of transitional housing programs where Susan lived after release from prison, until she absconded near the end of the year. When Susan wanted to discontinue group counseling, the officer wrote that she had given Susan this encouragement:

It is okay to be hurt with feedback, but the key is to stay in the game and keep moving. You have been out of prison for several months and made progress and avoided sanctions because you are still in the game.

Staff members at a transitional housing program wanted the supervising officer to sanction Susan, but instead the officer helped with additional services, a new residence, and concrete assistance in the form of bus passes.

For Susan, characteristic elements of Traditional County supervision were mixed with those typical of the gender-responsive approach. In contrast to the typical approach in Gender Responsive County, several case note entries focused on the officer's helping Susan correct her "thinking errors" and her "criminal thinking." Furthermore, Susan described a program that helped her, but confirmed the characteristic services gaps in Traditional County as she regretted that the program was just one hour a week. She also said it was "less intense than other programs, more relaxed for participants." Referrals to aftercare treatment, women's support groups, the self-esteem group, and other women-oriented support groups normally used in Gender Responsive County were absent.

WOMEN'S DECISIONS TO AVOID
INTERVENTIONS AND CHANGE

Even with broad and intense supervision, some women make choices that lead them back to crime and incarceration. Some simply abscond. Others are available for supervision, but resist its interventions and the requirements of other programs.

Absconding

In both counties, some women avoided contact. Supervising officers' various tactics to monitor the women and interact with them regularly — including home visits, required appointments, and drug testing — made little difference for some women. The discussion of housing in chapter 3 described women who changed housing constantly and noted that, for some, moving was an effective way to avoid supervision.

Women under supervision in multiple counties purposely created confusion by moving between counties, telling each authority that they were being supervised in another county. Women disconnected from family and residing in unstable housing easily relocate. When a Gender Responsive County supervising officer tried to locate a woman who lived in a trailer, she found the trailer missing and the lot "littered with syringes." Women moved from Gender Responsive County specifically to avoid its emphasis on residential substance abuse treatment. They moved from other counties with intensive supervision to another part of the state, or left the state entirely. In a few instances, women moved without permission seemingly in an effort to stop breaking the law, perhaps to get away from friends involved with drugs. They relocated to leave jobs — like bartending and exotic dancing — that exposed them to alcohol and sexual propositions. However, for the active drug users who failed, moving was usually a way to avoid supervision and treatment, especially in Gender Responsive County.

Resisting

Meredith serves as an example of the women who resisted offers of extensive services and intensive supervision in Gender Responsive County. Her supervising officer described a court hearing this way:

> In Court, I recommended six months residential drug treatment or six months in jail. Meredith turned to her supporters in the courtroom for advice. She told the judge she would take jail.

Others, like Barrie, stayed in the community but resisted intensive and sustained supervision. Barrie told the interviewer:

> I told the PO I had not wanted a job or a place to live since being on supervision and did the exact opposite of what they ask me to do. I have a problem with people telling me what to do. I like the fact that I can finish my jail time and be done with my supervision, and I don't have to report after I'm released from jail.

Although Barrie and women like her attend supervision and program meetings, interventions have no effect. Like Sheila, they resist pressure to desist from drug use and illegal behavior. Gender Responsive County supervised Sheila for ten years, during which she served several prison and jail terms. The supervising officer wrote that she "invited" Sheila to talk about residential treatment when Sheila mentioned a plan to run away due to her depression. The officer also sanctioned her with several days in jail for various violations. When Sheila's parents kept calling the officer to report continued drug use, the officer ordered her to the work release center, where she worked and participated in the Intensive Drug Treatment Program. At the year-end interview, Sheila told the interviewer that supervision had had no impact on her:

> Ain't nothing I like. I can't wait to get off and never see them again. I didn't like it at all. [No skills were] obtained so far.

Marilyn, from Gender Responsive County, felt her supervising officer harassed her, wanted her to come into the office at unreasonable times, took urine tests when "she has no right to," and required a three-hour substance abuse evaluation when Marilyn "did not have time to do that." Marilyn explained that Narcotics Anonymous had benefited her and taught her how to have healthy interactions, such as not yelling at her children. The self-help groups, she said, provided "supportive folks around so I have a chance of making it in my sobriety." But, when asked what she liked about Narcotics Anonymous, Marilyn named two features: the program is "noncommittal" and there is "nothing mandatory about the program." Some women resist and resent efforts to stop their drug use and to get them to comply with other conditions of supervision. Even extensive monitoring, referrals, and resources do not guarantee success. Resistant women cling to their identities as lawbreakers, resist supervision requirements, and avoid programming that pressures them to change.

SYSTEM INADEQUACIES

In both counties, women face waiting lists and inadequate resources for substance abuse treatment and housing. They wait in jail for openings in residential treatment programs. Leslie's Traditional County supervising officer noted his plan to sanction her only to keep her in the work release center when she faced homelessness upon release. However, even this desperate tactic failed. The work release center staff refused to keep her because she had a medical condition that they felt created a liability for the facility.

Extensive efforts by women, supervising officers, other professionals, and relatives cannot always prevent delays in getting women into substance abuse treatment. I present next examples from Gender Responsive County, where officers most often try to get women into residential treatment. The same problems stalled treatment in both counties, however. Audrey's history of violence created barriers to locating a substance abuse treatment program that would accept her. Lynne waited for an opening in treatment, but then failed to show up after being accepted. Meredith could not afford the recommended residential treatment program, so she waited to see if she qualified for state medical insurance. Most residential programs require that women not take legal psychotropic medications, such as Prozac or Xanax. That meant they had to either stop taking these prescribed drugs, or search out and wait for openings in the rare "dual diagnosis" or "co-occurring disorder" programs that accept women with both substance abuse and other mental health conditions (O'Brien and Young 2006; Veysey et al. 2005). Admission criteria, waiting lists, transportation problems for women in outpatient treatment, and problems with insurance block many women's entry into recommended substance abuse treatment.

Program access problems exist even in Gender Responsive County, where supervising officers form more ties within the network of treatment providers and make extensive referrals for different sorts of help. The result is that women do not receive the services they require to address their addictions and other needs. One underserved Gender Responsive County woman, Pat, began supervision after release from an inpatient substance abuse treatment program. She did not actually finish the recommended inpatient phase because, just before graduation, she was expelled for pulling a chair out from under another participant. In the early months of supervision, she avoided required outpatient treatment groups and continued using drugs. The supervising officer met some basic needs by providing clothing, deodorant, hair-care products, and bus passes. At one point, Pat agreed to a sanction of 120 days in the work release center. In the center, she attempted suicide twice, and according to case notes, "she almost died." Treatment staff told the officer that "she does not make sense, there may be some neurological problems," and that the "jail feels they have nothing else to offer her." The supervising officer thought Pat needed a neurological evaluation for suspected brain damage, but it was not arranged during the study year. A reading of case notes suggests that the officer could not find a source of funds to pay for the evaluation. After Pat's release from jail, the supervising officer could not locate her. In the tenth month of the year, the court issued a warrant for her arrest, and she was then officially considered to have absconded.

Crystal, also from Gender Responsive County, exhausted all program supports. For many years, she used methamphetamines, cocaine, and heroin. She told the supervising officer that she continued to use "crank [a form of crystallized methamphetamine] to keep me awake." She had completed a dual diagnosis program for people with mental health and substance abuse problems. Due to severe depression, she saw a mental health professional. Her medication made her shake, and she had uncontrolled diabetes. Several people told the officer that Crystal slept much of the time. The officer noted difficulty communicating with Crystal because she could not pay attention or respond. Arrested on old warrants, Crystal received a prison sentence during the year. The prison's substance abuse treatment staff decided her needs were beyond their capacity to treat, and they released Crystal early. Years of illness, drug use, mental illness, and taking medication intertwine to profoundly affect women like Crystal. The justice system is not equipped to provide or arrange for the help needed for women with such damaging histories.

Incarceration often had no positive impact. Ellen became a study participant after she was convicted for robbing a store clerk. She committed the robbery while on parole from prison for a burglary. During the year, she missed many appointments, refused required outpatient treatment, and repeatedly tested positive for cocaine. She served separate jail sanctions of fifteen, thirty, and ninety days for these acts and for a new theft charge. At the year-end interview, her only source of income was selling drugs. Ellen described the most helpful program as unrelated to supervision. Responding to an advertisement, she attended a drug treatment program that "kept me clean for a little while and was a place to detox." She said that unlike other programs, it did not pressure her to "tell them my business." In jail, Ellen did not participate in substance abuse treatment or prepare to enter residential treatment. Use of jail time as a transition to treatment was common practice in Gender Responsive County. Ellen, like Marilyn, preferred programs that did not challenge her identity and lifestyle and that required little personal engagement.

Some women felt that incarceration was helpful, but the data do not give supporting evidence. A woman in Gender Responsive County spent time in boot camp during the year, which she said helped by getting her to constantly examine her "criminal thinking." However, the program transferred her to prison for sexual contact with another participant and stealing medical supplies. The self-reported improvement in "criminal thinking" apparently did not prevent her from stealing or breaking program rules. Other women with revoked supervision told interviewers that jail and prison programs had changed them for the better. Since they were still incarcerated at the end of the year, I cannot determine whether the change affected their drug use or lawbreaking after release.

DISCUSSION OF SUPERVISION AND
FAILURE IN THE TWO COUNTIES

On the surface, the numbers suggest that similar proportions of substance-centered women failed in each county. Closer examination of detailed, qualitative data clarifies that Traditional County supervision tactics promoted failure. In contrast, women's choices in combination with gaps in needed resources and programs, not supervision tactics, account for failure in Gender Responsive County. For instance, Gender Responsive County stresses the links among substance use monitoring, professional evaluation, treatment, reevaluation in response to continued drug use, and placement in increasingly intense residential settings. Yet the progression may be stalled due to waiting lists, admission criteria, and lack of insurance.

The gender-responsive ideal that Gender Responsive County attempts to implement alters the nature of supervision. Gender-responsive supervision routinely addresses myriad gender-related needs. Supervising officers' relationships with clients take different forms in the two counties. Even those women who officially fail probation and parole in Gender Responsive County express appreciation toward their supervising officers. Compared to women in Traditional County, those in Gender Responsive County less often temper their statements about how officers "helped" with the qualification that the help was not quite enough. Evidence in later chapters confirms and further explains the effectiveness of gender-responsive supervision.

5

Supervision for Women
Using Drugs but Not Failing

The PO seems to only want to catch women doing something
wrong instead of helping. There is no real communication.
BETH, Traditional County

I couldn't be happier in learning about myself. I'm learning
how to live life on life's terms. I'm complete.
NORA, Gender Responsive County

This chapter focuses on substance-centered women who used drugs for at least some part of the year, but did not commit new crimes. To some degree they are making it, because at year's end, they are not absconded or incarcerated. Like Beth, quoted above, many substance-centered women making it in Traditional County view supervision negatively. Like Nora, also quoted above, many Gender Responsive County women view supervision very positively. Regardless of their views of probation or parole, these women made it to the end of the year with some success. Some were briefly sent to jail or the work release center, and some violated supervision requirements. Still, this group avoided new charges and incarceration (see chapter 3).

Substance-centered Gender Responsive County women were slightly more likely to make it than their counterparts in Traditional County (57.8 percent of 109 women in Gender Responsive County, and 53.8 percent of 132 women in Traditional County). Showing a greater difference, the proportion of Gender Responsive County women engaged in substance abuse treatment was much higher than the proportion in Traditional County (89.3 percent of twenty-eight women in Gender Responsive County, and 50 percent of twenty women in Traditional County). The path to treatment varied. Supervising officers ordered some women into specific programs, while other women drew on personal contacts or found programs on their own initiative. Still others were assisted by relatives and medical insurance companies. The imminent loss of child custody motivated some women to enter programs.

There were women who struggled with supervising officers over starting and completing drug treatment throughout the year. These women experienced few positive changes—that is, they reported no new insights, education, or jobs. For others, treatment programs triggered numerous positive changes in resources, child custody, intimate partners, and self. Specific supervision tactics affected whether, how, and where women engaged in substance abuse treatment. Gender Responsive County supervising officers used tactics that effectively prompt treatment, resulting in more women's receiving treatment in that county.

WOMEN MANAGING ON THEIR OWN
IN TRADITIONAL COUNTY

Because Traditional County supervision tends to be minimal, women may appear to successfully complete supervision while in fact continuing to break the law and without making lifestyle or personal changes to resist drug use and crime. Incomplete information based on minimal supervision creates the incorrect impression that the women are doing well. Deb is one of many Traditional County women in this category. She showed indication of continued drug use, but little other information and little supervision can be found in the sparse case notes. The notes indicate that she admitted using marijuana before her first meeting with her supervising officer, and that the officer denied her request to visit a "known gang member" in prison. After the first visit, Deb contacted her supervisor through the mail and phone calls. She reported holding a temporary job and attending substance abuse counseling. Since the officer did not carry out drug testing or meet face-to-face again with Deb, it is not known whether her reports are true.

Traditional County officers do not request extensions when cases expire, which contributes to the high proportion of women under limited supervision. Eddie reported monthly after her case was transferred from another state. The expiration date, set by the other state, had arrived, but the Traditional County officer knew that Eddie had multiple problems.

Eddie failed to complete her community supervision and submit for drug testing. She delayed treatment for her methamphetamine addiction, because she lacked insurance for the required substance abuse evaluation. Eddie worried about one daughter who was pregnant, and another whom she described as "out of control." The formal expiration date drove the supervising officer's decision to end probation. By contrast, in Gender Responsive County, failure to meet supervision conditions or undetermined and unaddressed needs typically led to an extension of supervision.

The previous chapter described Traditional County supervising officers' chronicling numerous troubles without interventions. The case notes reveal the same pattern for Traditional County women managing in the community. Colette's supervising officer wrote that in the fourth month of her supervision, she was trying to "detox off methadone." With expired insurance, she could not afford the $225 monthly cost for methadone. Substance abuse treatment staff advised the officer that she was cutting back too quickly. When Colette tested positive for cocaine, she told the officer she had used with a friend from work; the officer simply told her to change jobs. A few weeks later, the officer sanctioned her with six days in jail for driving with a suspended license. For the next few months, Colette resumed taking a higher dose of methadone. According to a case note, she was worried about getting the money she owed for the methadone. In the tenth month of supervision, Colette got a job as the assistant manager at a restaurant, found a better place to live, and continued taking methadone. The next month, the officer reduced supervision to mailed reports. The supervising officer did nothing to address Colette's shortage of funds for methadone. Furthermore, the officer's directive to change jobs to get away from a drug-using co-worker could have exacerbated Colette's financial difficulties.

Despite limited help from supervising officers, some Traditional County women — using resources provided by relatives, friends, programs, or churches, or through their own devices — engaged in substance abuse treatment. They experienced positive changes in their lives and remained in the community without new arrests. A degree of nonintervention did not prevent them from finishing the year with some success.

The women in this group vary in their assessment of the limited and narrow supervision they received. Beth felt very differently from the women in Gender Responsive County, saying that her Traditional County supervising officer denied the validity of her feelings. When she said she felt intimidated by the officer, the officer responded: "[It is] just in your mind." The interviewer added this comment on the data collection form: "The participant found absolutely nothing useful about her experience on supervision." In Gender Responsive County, supervising officers and special groups—for example, the self-esteem group and the grief group—emphasized attention to women's feelings.

Several Traditional County women actually praised the lack of intervention. One told the interviewer she liked "being put on mail in [monthly reporting by mail] sooner than expected." She disliked "having to come here every month for basically nothing" because "I was already taking care of my drug problem." She felt that it was "up to me to change and the PO did not help me with my problems."

Ida also preferred Traditional County's limited supervision. She said: "I liked that I was on the limited supervision. I never saw the PO in the first place." Just before the start of limited supervision, Ida ignored a letter instructing her to meet with substance abuse providers. Five months later, the officer indicated there was "no reason not to allow" Ida's visit with a man in prison, because she was on the limited supervision caseload. Ironically, limited supervision itself provided the rationale for further reducing restrictions on Ida. Subsequent case notes, however, suggest continued involvement with drugs and crime. Ida's mother reported unusual behavior and suspicions of drug use to the supervising officer. A week later, her father called to say he had tapes of Ida "attempting to make drug deals and speaking of someone hitting her child." The supervising officer noted advising the father to contact the police. In another week's time, the officer wrote that Ida said "there were no problems." In Traditional County, nonintervention minimizes state intrusions into women's personal lives. It also limits supervising officers' knowledge of the women, as well as their efforts to increase access to resources.

WOMEN STRUGGLING TO GET DRUG TREATMENT IN GENDER RESPONSIVE COUNTY

Interaction between supervising officers and women sometimes produces a yearlong struggle over entering and completing substance abuse treatment. Most of the women in the study who engaged in this struggle were from Gender Responsive County.

I have already described the multiple steps and barriers to substance abuse treatment. The process and the barriers are the same for the women considered in this chapter. In Gender Responsive County especially, supervising officers invest heavily in getting women over the barriers that kept them from the particular programs recommended by professional substance abuse evaluators. This involvement starts with the decision to supervise Gender Responsive County women at higher levels than indicated by the statewide risk assessment system. Officers' rationales for this approach seem contradictory, as they cite both first-time offending and having a long history of contact with the justice system. For example, one Gender Responsive County supervising officer wrote: "First time on probation, meth user needs to be closely monitored the first six months." Another wrote: "Twenty-one-year old heroin addict, no employment skills, needs resources of the parole and probation program." Consistent with the recurring theme that county differences are a matter of degree rather than absolutes, in Traditional County, officers increased supervision of a few substance-centered women — for example, because of serious mental health problems. However, increased supervision for a variety of different reasons was much more common in Gender Responsive County.

Supervising officers' efforts, women's vacillating willingness to enter and complete programs, and numerous barriers to evaluation and placement contribute to the struggle over treatment. The struggle can take a year or even longer. Nancy's evolving situation epitomizes the struggle in Gender Responsive County. She was initially supervised at a higher level than indicated by her risk score, because the officer wanted to know "why she and her partner were out stealing when there was a child with them." During a home visit three weeks after supervision began, the officer saw fresh track marks on Nancy's arms and required a substance abuse evaluation. Nancy missed the first appointment but later was evaluated, went to a detoxification program, and enrolled in a residential treatment program where her child could live, too.

After being transferred to outpatient treatment, Nancy missed group meetings and took drugs. The supervising officer tried to get her into another program. However, Nancy had to be admitted to a detoxification program for five days first, because she had to be clean to begin residential treatment. She missed one appointment to enter detox, moved in, but then left. The supervising officer noted that Nancy said she left because the program was "a zoo," and the children were "out of control." Nancy told the supervising officer she could redo the residential and outpatient programs she had failed to complete before, and the officer noted: "I put her back on the UA [urine analysis] calendar." Nancy never started the program. She repeatedly tested positive for heroin and cocaine. These case notes and those that follow provide a detailed picture of how hard it is to coordinate an extremely complicated set of factors. The common elements include the addicted woman's wavering desire for detoxification and treatment; the availability of appropriate detoxification, substance abuse evaluations, and treatment; insurance and child-care needs; and pressure on mothers to support their children.

Nancy definitely wanted substance abuse treatment. After eight months of supervision and admitted heroin use, she expressed the desire to go to an all-woman program to get well. She entered the jail-based intensive substance abuse treatment program, where staff immediately transferred her to a detox center because she had drugs in her system. The substance abuse counselor at the jail-based detox program felt she needed more intensive treatment than they could provide. The waiting lists for appropriate programs were over two months long. Thus, after completing the detoxification program, Nancy moved back in with her mother to wait for an opening. Several weeks later, she told the officer she no longer wanted intensive treatment. She subsequently left her mother's home, and neither her mother nor the officer could find her. By the time she again changed her mind, the substance abuse evaluation had expired. Nancy missed appointments for a new evaluation. A required physical examination further delayed the substance abuse evaluation. Then there were no openings in the evaluation schedule. The supervising officer described a phone message from Nancy:

> She says she has been at the office to have a substance abuse assessment every day. She has to go in the morning to the Case Management Program to get a physical before they will transfer her to the place for the assessment. After that, she is going to sit at the assessment place and see if they can squeeze her in today. If they cannot, she does not have an appointment until Monday.

Finally, two months after attempting to enter more intense treatment than the jail-based program, Nancy told the supervising officer she wanted to go to jail instead of treatment. She specified days and times when the officer could pick her up and transport her to jail.

A few days later, at her mother's urging, Nancy changed her mind and indicated yet again that she wanted treatment. She was cleared for an evaluation by the Case Management Program, but the obstacle course created by waiting lists and insurance processes continued to block her entry. The evaluation program could not schedule an appointment for several days, but she could go every day and they would attempt to "get her in." Two months later, with a current evaluation, Nancy started the recommended intense substance abuse program. But, on the day she entered, she was discharged due to severe withdrawal symptoms. The counselors stated that if she returned after detox and was "clean," she could start again. She restarted the program and was there at the end of the year. At the twelve-month interview, Nancy said the residential treatment program suggested by the supervising officer helped the most. It taught "coping skills, time management and responsibility." It showed her "how to stay drug free, to be responsible for my own actions."

Nancy was involved in struggle to get into treatment on multiple levels. She battled herself, wavering in her decision to enter residential treatment. She struggled with her mother, who pressured her to get treatment. To get her into treatment, the supervising officer contended with Nancy and with program availability, protocols, and decisions. All parties, including treatment providers and agents in the justice system, worked hard to get Nancy past the waiting lists, to provide appropriate insurance and an up-to-date substance abuse evaluation, and to get her clean enough to enter the right sort of a program.

The supervising officer played a crucial role in Nancy's entering and staying at a recommended program. The officer was persistent, making home visits, office appointments, and phone calls; conversed at length with Nancy; used threats; and coordinated with substance abuse evaluators and treatment program staff, as well as Nancy's mother. Despite delays and obstacles, the officer got Nancy into a recommended program. Although Nancy hesitated at times, she also persisted in the end.

Programs often expel women for at least a while when they have a positive drug test or violate other program requirements and rules. One woman said a program terminated her because she refused to admit the degree to which she had hurt other people through her substance abuse. When women are expelled, the entire admission process begins again, since insurance might have expired, detoxification might be needed, new evaluations might be required, and alternative programs must be identified. Time spent on new waiting lists, problems with new programs and past residential treatment, and difficulties locating aftercare treatment are all real possibilities. Gender Responsive County supervisors dedicate considerable time to managing the process of accessing treatment.

A similar but qualitatively different pattern of struggle is found for a small proportion of Traditional County substance-centered women. During the year of supervision, Annette, a participant in a pilot program with special intensive supervision, moved from one treatment program to another. At the first interview, she reported having recently used cocaine and methamphetamines. She thought she needed treatment for methamphetamines. Shortly after supervision began, she was asked to leave a residential treatment program that her supervising officer had helped her enter. In the third month of supervision, when she could not be located, the supervising officer issued a warrant for her arrest. Using the protocol typical of Gender Responsive County, the Traditional County officer called for her to spend thirty days in jail and then go to an alternative residential treatment program. In the sixth month of supervision, Annette wanted intensive outpatient treatment, but her supervising officer ordered her to residential treatment. After a few weeks, the residential treatment program terminated Annette as a client. The officer then located another residential program. Ready to graduate two months later, Annette had no place to live. Up to this point, the Traditional County officer had taken actions similar to those commonly found in Gender Responsive County.

Then, contrary to Gender Responsive County practice, a new Traditional County supervisor took over Annette's case because she moved to transitional housing in a different zip code area. The transitional housing did not work out. The new supervising officer chronicled Annette's troubles. First Annette moved in with her stepfather, but, due to loyalty, moved out after discovering her mother had a restraining order against him. Annette's mother and her new partner refused her request to live with them. After that, Annette lived for short periods at various friends' residences. The new supervising officer arrested her for smoking marijuana. Traditional County supervision is qualitatively different from supervision in Gender Responsive County. It does not consistently provide a relationship with one supervising officer. Except for Annette's time in the pilot project of intensive supervision, officers chronicled her evolving problems but did not directly intervene until making an arrest for noncompliance with supervision conditions.

Very common supervision tactics in Gender Responsive County are brief jail sanctions when women use drugs, and the use of jail terms to get women clean enough to enter residential treatment. Required living arrangements can also be tactics. Women may be required to live in jail or the work release center because they have no options, or in order to attend the Intensive Drug Treatment Program. Officers coordinate with staff at shelters and transitional housing to help homeless women. Although substance-centered women may be referred to multiple services, most who are struggling with getting into treatment do not actually use a wide range of other services. Their time and energy and those of their supervising officers are consumed with overcoming obstacles to treatment. As I highlighted in the last chapter, whether women ended the year still struggling to obtain substance abuse treatment depended in part on their own actions. It also depended on whether supervising officers continued to work on behalf of the women to get them into what may become a series of substance abuse treatment programs interspersed with brief sanctions, including jail stays, as a response to relapses back into drug use.

THE PROLIFERATION OF POSITIVE CHANGES

Women who move beyond the struggle over treatment experience numerous positive changes in their lives and in themselves. They stop living in places with easy access to drugs. Some stop using drugs entirely. As they cut drug use, they reconnect with noncriminal family members, engage in educational programs, prepare for employment, and start working. They attend parenting programs, and a few keep or regain child custody. Developing a relationship with a partner who is not drug-centered or abusive is another possible change.

The women in this study described benefits from groups and treatment, including support, structure, learning, referrals, and advocacy. They developed positive self-perceptions, learned to think problems through, and gained decision-making skills. These benefits came from relationships with supervising officers, primarily those in Gender Responsive County, and with substance abuse treatment staff, counselors, social workers, psychologists, and lawyers. They also resulted from interactions with peers in treatment groups. How did some women get past drug-centered lifestyles and relationships, and the challenges of getting into and completing substance abuse treatment? How did they come to experience positive relationships, settings, and internal changes?

Most often, full engagement in a substance abuse treatment program precedes other changes. First, women get clean, then they leave abusive and criminal partners, acquire law-abiding partners, develop noncriminal support networks, and obtain education and work skills. Some find work and advance in their careers. This sequence of events occurs in part because women who stop using drugs are motivated and able to find and keep partners who do not use drugs. They actively want to leave drug-using partners. Judy, supervised in Gender Responsive County, made the positive changes that stem from engaging in substance abuse treatment. By the end of the study, she had earned her GED. A relative offered financial assistance until her job search proved fruitful. Also, she arranged a stable housing situation, rooming with another participant in her substance abuse treatment program. She successfully completed parole. In a pattern that other researchers also document, internal perceptions and motivations cause offenders to begin to desire, and then to find, prosocial social networks (Giordano, Cernkovich, and Holland 2003). In a few cases, women in the study who used drugs during the year, but otherwise were law-abiding, experienced positive changes before they stopped using drugs. However, in most cases, a series of positive changes started with substance abuse treatment that promoted abstinence from drugs; subsequently, there were both internal and external beneficial changes.

As would be expected, given the higher emphasis in Gender Responsive County on women's relationships with supervising officers and entry into treatment, the counties differ in terms of multiple positive changes for women. In Gender Responsive County, 66.7 percent (eighteen of twenty-seven) of active users who were making it participated in substance abuse treatment programs and had subsequent, multiple positive changes. In Traditional County, 35 percent (seven of twenty) of women followed this pattern of treatment's leading to positive changes of many types. Supervising officers affected the process differently in the two counties. Most Gender Responsive County women (77.8 percent, or fourteen of eighteen) who took part in substance abuse treatment did so at least partly because of a supervising officer's actions. This was the case for a lower percentage (28.6 percent, or two of seven) of Traditional County women.

When the supervising officer's actions do not account for a woman's involvement in substance abuse treatment, other forces do. Selected women in both counties entered substance abuse treatment more as a response to the imminent loss of child custody than because of supervision. The supervising officer's monitoring of substance use may have had some impact, but for a few women in Gender Responsive County, grandparents' threats to "take children away" or Child and Family Services Agency involvement seemed to be the key antecedents. Similarly, a Traditional County woman with previous treatment failures finally succeeded in residential treatment after Child and Family Services gave her a "last chance" to regain child custody. Although many substance-centered women had support networks completely populated by friends, family members, and partners involved with crime and drugs, this was not the case for all the women. Pressure and resources from family members provided them with impetus to get treatment that would stimulate positive change. Nancy's mother's efforts, described above—combined with the supervising officer's actions—pushed Nancy to enter treatment. For other women, relatives or personal motivation caused them to enter treatment.

For Native American women, tribal resources provide access to a comprehensive network of treatment and other programs. In the study setting, the tribes deliver comprehensive residential and outpatient substance abuse treatment. Programs assist women's children and other relatives. Waiting lists and lack of access to medical insurance do not pose serious barriers. The tribal programs also link women to housing, job training, and work opportunities.

The elements of supervision that make a difference are: a high level of scrutiny; wraparound services and a continuum of care; increased monitoring, sanctions, and treatment requirements in response to drug use; supervising officers' ties to community-based programs and professionals; and women's relationships with supervising officers. Many of these elements typify the gender-responsive approach to corrections. Analysis and discussion of these elements show how Gender Responsive County generates positive effects.

SUCCESS WITH BROAD AND INTENSE SUPERVISION
FOR SUBSTANCE-CENTERED WOMEN

Detailed information about the substance-centered women who experienced some success during the year both confirms and adds details to the findings about those who failed. It shows how broadly targeted help and referrals support the women's engagement in treatment and many other positive changes. It also shows the scrutiny that supervising officers apply to women's lives, and the intrusiveness of the most extreme monitoring, sanctions, and treatment requirements. The substance-centered women who achieved some success had complicated relationships and strong connections to their supervising officers. Finally, the data confirm the importance of delivering supervision as part of a web of interconnected programs.

Sequencing Help and Referrals for Multiple Problems

Gender Responsive County officers assess and meet a very wide range of women's needs. Just as they provided help for women who failed, officers provided basic material and financial resources for those who made it to the end of the year. Women receive bus tickets for job searches and items from a clothing and toiletries supply in the community corrections offices. If women's clothes are unsuitable for interviews or work, officers hand out vouchers for use at a low-cost clothing store. Community supervision offices make down payments at Oxford Houses, as well as deposits or partial payments for substance abuse treatment programs. Women do not have to pay this money back if they succeed in the program. In contrast, reducing supervision to a limited level or ending it to reduce or eliminate fees is the common way to provide financial assistance in Traditional County. In Gender Responsive County, material help increases when supervision is at a fairly high level, but in Traditional County, the most common material help actually requires reducing or stopping supervision.

By considering, talking about, and making referrals for a broad set of troubles that change over time, Gender Responsive County officers deliver wraparound services and provide a continuum of care. This is evident in the case of Nora, who started the year using methamphetamine, but told her supervising officer she did not have a drug problem. Later, she told the officer she was making money "running drugs," and she could not stop "using the needle." At that point, the officer ignored her request to go to outpatient treatment and gave her two choices: participate in the Intensive Drug Treatment Program while living at the work release center, or let the judge decide her fate. Choosing the work release center, Nora found a job making $9 an hour and completed the in-house phase of substance abuse treatment. She told the officer she was afraid to be released because a drug house was her only option for a residence. Before housing could be arranged, she absconded. She joined up with a man who used methamphetamines, and she briefly left the state. On her return, she called her supervising officer to say she was "sick of worrying about the police." The officer advised her that her chances of alternative sanctions (i.e., drug treatment with no incarceration) were higher if she turned herself in, which she did. After Nora spent a short time in jail, the officer arranged for her to enter a residential substance abuse treatment program.

Nora's sequential use of different resources shows how Gender Responsive County helps create change in women and their lives. The continuum of care was broken when Nora had no housing following the Intensive Drug Treatment Program. This preceded and probably precipitated her absconding. Because of the nature of her relationship with the supervising officer, Nora felt able to call for help. The expectation that drug use will likely be met with increased substance abuse treatment rather than incarceration leaves the door open for women to ask for help and to reveal drug use. Even though she was arrested, Nora spent just a short time in jail before she entered residential treatment, which she said led to numerous internal changes. She told the interviewer she had learned "how to identify my feelings and deal with them on a mature level. When I feel angry, [I learned] to take time out, breathe and examine my part in the event."

During the year, the supervising officer pulled together different programs and resources to support Nora's multiple positive changes. According to the case notes, the officer called the Community Mental Health Agency to check on a drug evaluation appointment time, and also checked on an appointment with the Employment Services Agency counselor. Nora told the officer that since she was not high all the time, she had especially strong feelings of anger and frustration. The officer responded by referring Nora to an anger management program. Later she channeled her into a substance abuse treatment program. In the end, as quoted at the beginning of this chapter, Nora told the interviewer:

I believe that I am getting everything I need here [at the residential treatment program]. I couldn't be happier in learning about myself. I'm learning how to live life on life's terms. I'm complete.

We cannot know whether Nora's feeling of "completeness" came from the consistent involvement of the supervising officer, the range of issues addressed in the final residential treatment program, services provided throughout the year, Nora's own efforts, or some combination of influences. However, Nora did say that she had benefited from a holistic approach, which made her feel "complete." Through her relationship with Nora, despite system inadequacies, the supervising officer provided continuity and access to intensive intervention.

Mary Ellen, a Native American woman in Gender Responsive County, also kept her supervising officer informed about her life, and the officer responded to multiple problems as they surfaced. Mary Ellen disclosed that before her conviction, she had been clean and sober for eight years. When she met her ex-boyfriend at a club, they used methamphetamines together. Then, Mary Ellen said, "I checked myself into a program." She stopped using drugs and moved in with a relative. Angry that Mary Ellen spent money from bottle returns on cigarettes instead of buying food for her child, the relative physically attacked her. Although she had no income or place to live, Mary Ellen left. She faced a long waiting list at the residential substance abuse treatment program to which she applied. She and her child spent several nights sleeping in her car in front of a sibling's house. She said she could not live with her sibling and his spouse because they were alcoholics. Her supervising officer had her make a call from the community supervision office to a shelter, where she found an opening. Because the shelter closed once winter ended, Mary Ellen applied to another shelter. She met the supervising officer's requirement to apply for state medical insurance and undergo substance abuse evaluation. Based on the evaluation, she was admitted to a sixty-day residential program with a Native American emphasis and was able to move there with her child in just ten days.

The supervising officer pointed out useful resources, made sure Mary Ellen applied for insurance, and helped her obtain a substance abuse evaluation. The substance abuse evaluation enabled Mary Ellen to access the tribe's resources and the residential program. During an interview, Mary Ellen gave an account of the supervising officer's help:

She has been on my ass, keeping me clean, getting my head together and getting back on my feet. When I was first homeless, she offered the use of the office phone and let me use the number for messages. She gave me supplies. She gave me bus tickets so I would not be tempted to drive the car [with no license]. She gives good advice.

In addition to the concrete help and limit setting, Mary Ellen's case highlights the positive impact of women's relationships with supervising officers in Gender Responsive County. In a later section, I will explore the nature of these relationships more fully.

Gender Responsive County officers demand that women be "honest" and that they access several programs and services. The officers mix tough demands and requirements with responsiveness to a range of troubles. Mary Anne, whose lengthy history of drug use is discussed in chapter 2, described this attention to multiple needs as helping with "all levels of a person." Judy also described her experience with a combination of interventions. She said the substance abuse treatment program she attended helped her the most, "because the staff members try to consider your personal background, family. From a woman's view they really worked with me, [and did] not just throw me away." She compared her supervision to prior supervision in another county:

The women at [Gender Responsive County] didn't let up. You can't continue manipulating them. They take care of business. They are really on top of it. [In the other county,] they have so many people they don't pay attention.

Some treatment programs provide women with multiple types of help beyond supervising officers' efforts. In Traditional County, a relative helped Mackenzie enter a life skills program. Mackenzie said this program helped her because it "dealt with the emotional, physical, spiritual — all levels of me." Gender Responsive County women described similar holistic programs, especially residential substance abuse treatment. Describing the program she finished, Mary Anne listed several things she learned: "parenting skills, discipline, how to be more understanding of developmental stages, how to talk about puberty and sex, how to look for signs of sexual abuse, nutritional needs, how to eat without gaining weight, how to handle myself in high risk situations, saying no to drug dealers." In chapter 3, I emphasized that women are situated at different points in a unique life course and in complex criminal and noncriminal support networks. The most effective programs avoid fragmentation. By responding on "all levels," they make women feel "complete." They never "throw them away."

Scrutiny and Increased Monitoring, Sanctions, and Treatment

Diana's situation illustrates how a high level of supervision can help identify needs. The courts convicted Diana of automobile theft. Like other Gender Responsive County women, Diana was supervised at a level higher than required for just one theft conviction. The officer wanted to know more about Diana, since this was her first time on probation. After drug testing revealed methamphetamine use, the supervising officer required a brief stay in jail so Diana could begin the Intensive Drug Treatment Program, followed by continued outpatient treatment, self-help groups, and electronic monitoring.

The term *early strike* captures the quick and forceful nature of Gender Responsive County officers to drug-using women. Early strikes are possible only if supervision levels start out and stay high. Officers use common tactics to gather considerable information on women. They pat them down during home and office visits, find drugs or drug paraphernalia, and immediately take women into custody. For first-time offenders in particular, Traditional County officers did not provide such intense and early intervention.

The home visit plays a crucial role in accomplishing high levels of supervision. It allows direct communication with relatives and observation of the physical state of women and their children, as well as household members' lifestyles. During home visits, officers search through closets, refrigerators, and cabinets for drugs, drug paraphernalia, and alcohol. They observe whether women are highly agitated or have sores on their faces or needle marks — signs of substance abuse. In Gender Responsive County, the signs trigger evaluation and increased treatment requirements. Home visits also confirm women's actual place of residence. Because so many substance-centered women move repeatedly and report false addresses, supervising officers use residence information as an indicator of probable drug use.

When women continue using drugs and refuse required treatment, Gender Responsive County supervising officers draw from a large array of increasingly intrusive and controlling responses. Initially, they warn women, assign them community service hours, or require participation on offender work crews on the weekends. They order women to submit to scheduled urinalysis tests and to attend outpatient treatment. Officers may escalate requirements to include random drug testing and increased hours of participation in outpatient treatment. If women continue to use drugs, officers insist on the most severe responses: electronic surveillance, residential substance abuse treatment, or sending women to jail or the work release center for substance abuse treatment in the Intensive Drug Treatment Program. A typical sequence of sanctions for continued drug use includes a day or two on a work crew, one night in jail, two days in jail, a week in jail, required participation in a residential treatment program, participation in the Intensive Drug Treatment Program while living at the work release center, and, finally, jail time followed by admission to a long-term residential treatment facility. Supervising officers orchestrate the women's movement through this sequence of graduated treatments and sanctions. They develop relationships with the women, convince them to accept sanctions, charge them with violations, and warn them of and then initiate revocations.

Laura experienced a graduated escalation in treatment and control in Gender Responsive County. Laura and her husband had operated a home-based meth lab before their convictions. Laura's supervising officer prohibited her from seeing her husband after his release from the men's section of the work release center. When Laura admitted to continued methamphetamine use, the officer sanctioned her to jail on her days off from work, told her to resume treatment, and required random drug testing. When she used again, the supervising officer told Laura to call her treatment program and leave a message that she had relapsed. The officer warned that one more positive test would lead to a jail sentence. Laura had to enroll in the Intensive Drug Treatment Program and wear "the bracelet" (be monitored electronically). Laura moved away from drug-using friends and lived with her grandmother. She viewed random drug testing as "helping me deal with my addiction." She praised the Intensive Drug Treatment Program, where "it was good to talk about things" in therapy. Although she wanted to take "the bracelet" off and end restrictive scheduling to attend programs, she felt that "it's there for a good reason. It's the most restrictive. Basically, it's house arrest. It's not what they call it, but it is."

As long as women use drugs, Gender Responsive County supervising officers consistently and repeatedly escalate a combination of monitoring, punishments, and treatment. Traditional County officers do sometimes refer women to residential treatment programs, but officers often allow women who keep using drugs to continue with outpatient treatment. At some point, officers in Traditional County abruptly send some women to jail with no plan for future treatment.

The array of options used in Gender Responsive County benefits women by preserving their strengths and resources, even while increasing monitoring, sanctions, and treatment. For example, Joanne had completed three years of college and was doing fairly well in the job market. When she continued to use drugs, the supervising officer assigned her to the Intensive Drug Treatment Program as a resident in the work release center, so she could continue working. Betty and her husband had an agreement that she could live with him and their children only when she was not using drugs. During the year, she used heroin heavily. The supervising officer explained that she did not make an arrest because "[I] believe a treatment approach versus taking her straight to jail is most effective." After some time on a waiting list, Betty began a methadone maintenance program. By the end of the year, she had been clean for two months, and she rejoined her family. The officer chose a sanction that allowed Betty to continue working and that did not separate her from her partner, who was a positive influence.

THE IMPACTS OF RELATIONSHIPS
WITH SUPERVISING OFFICERS

Consistently demanding honesty, in Gender Responsive County, officers expect women to divulge their drug use. They "invite" women to be open and honest. They repeatedly "ask for the truth." Early in her year of supervision, according to Joanne, the officer ordered her to live at the work release center for four days "because I was untruthful with my PO." Women who admit to violating probation conditions receive less severe sanctions than those who lie. This is reflected in Gender Responsive County case notes, which include several examples of women's calling their supervising officers to ask for help or advice. The women realize that if they are honest, officers reciprocate by focusing more on treatment than on sanctions. In addition, officers punish women not just for using drugs, but also for lying about it.

Many Gender Responsive County women describe wholly positive relationships with supervising officers. Mary Ellen identified supervision as the program that helped her the most. She appreciated "not being treated by the past but by who I am now." Maggie said:

> Supervision was helpful overall, since it taught me I do not need to rely on drugs to satisfy my needs, and there is a better world out there without drugs. I like the honesty of the program. The PO taught me that a drug addiction is a sickness, and there is a way to get well. It does not make you a bad person.

Julie explained that compared to previous supervision, Gender Responsive County is better because "it is more flexible and personal." She most liked that "the PO wants people to succeed." Diana said the officer was "kind and very understanding with my life." Kelly described her supervising officer:

> She is a real likable personality like a regular person who really cares about me. She's not a goody goody either. My present PO is really concerned and nice, but still very stern and firm, really good! In the past they have been harsh and cold, and there has been no follow up. When I was in jail or treatment [past POs] were glad I was out of their hair for a while and were impossible to reach.

Common themes in the positive comments are: supervising officers got to know women, responded to them as unique and valued individuals, heard and accepted their feelings as valid, maintained the relationship over time, and were both supportive and stern. The mixture of support and "being on my ass" was viewed positively. Consistent with other researchers' findings, effective relationships between probation officers and clients are characterized by a mixture of caring with controls (Skeem et al. 2009 and 2007). The data from the present study show the central role of relationships between women and supervising officers in accomplishing this mixture. At least some women experience a high level of supervision as positive and helpful, rather than as controlling and intrusive.

Frequently, women in Gender Responsive County are ambivalent: they appreciate the quality of their relationships with officers, but they want either more attention or less control and direction. Mary Anne expressed such ambivalence, saying her officer was "too busy" to give her adequate time, but noting that she "has a caring heart but she has a firm hand, a good combination of caring but also setting strong boundaries." An earlier paragraph quoted Kelly's positive description of her relationship with the supervising officer. She also contradicts her own positive assessment:

> [I do not like] having to go to treatment when I don't want to, or to get feedback about my roommate, kids, and so on. I get feedback when I don't want it. I have to tell the PO everything. The worst part of the program is the loss of control, having to tell the PO everything about boyfriends and other things.

Some women in both counties describe entirely negative relationships with supervising officers. This is most common in Traditional County. The preponderance of information from the study suggests that in Gender Responsive County, the women value open communication, acceptance, and positive relationships, though they may be ambivalent about the degree of oversight and control. Many Traditional County women see officers as solely concerned with enforcing conditions of supervision and monitoring them, not helping them.

COMMUNITY SUPERVISION
IN A WEB OF PROGRAMS

Gender Responsive County supervision is integrated with external agencies and programs, has its own counseling and support groups, and provides coordinated supervision for intimate partners who are also on probation or parole. Gender Responsive County officers use coordinated supervision to address couples' child support issues. They also use coordinated supervision to enforce court orders that prohibit contact between partners, or between a parent and children. They carry out joint home visits and execute outstanding warrants. Staff in external agencies and programs share information and coordinate with the supervising officers. These agencies include Community Mental Health and myriad outpatient and residential substance abuse treatment programs. As I mentioned in the introduction, a designated staff member from the Employment Services Agency works in the community supervision office on certain days. The self-esteem group, grief group, and woman's support group are all part of Gender Responsive County's community supervision. When supervising officers meet as a team, external agency staff and internal group leaders participate in discussions about the women under supervision. In addition to formal meetings, supervising officers and other professionals communicate through considerable face-to-face interaction and phone contacts. When services are confidential — for example, mental health or substance abuse treatment counseling — staff obtain written permission from women to allow information sharing.

Sometimes the professional support network of people, including the supervising officer, coordinates to counteract partner or peer pressure on women to stop treatment and continue drug use. According to case notes, Paula's partner pressured her not to go to counseling and self-help groups and made plans that interfered with her attendance. At a self-esteem group meeting, she said that this man created so much stress that she had consumed drugs and alcohol. Consistent with practice in Gender Responsive County, the self-esteem group leader told the supervising officer that Paula had "relapsed." Paula's supervising officer increased the level of supervision and required her to attend extra Alcoholics Anonymous and Narcotics Anonymous meetings. Paula felt that the group meetings "kept me clean and it's been recovery support because I get to see other addicts stay clean that are in the program applying twelve steps to life in general." She described the benefits of the self-esteem group, which was "part of supervision [and which] tells you how to deal with things when you're real upset." Supervising officers connect women to multiple community services and programs that counteract the negative influences that surround them.

CONTRASTING THE EXTREMES
IN SUPERVISION TACTICS

Combined analysis of substance-centered women who used drugs during the year and who either failed or made it clarifies in some detail two models of supervision. Limited and narrow supervision tactics characterize Traditional County:

· Use of low and reduced levels of supervision for reasons including the objective scoring system, completion of a residential treatment program, desire to reduce a women's fees for supervision, or the lack of violence involved in the offense.

- Not unusual for known drug users to have no drug testing.
- For women who continue using drugs, no escalation in monitoring, controls, or treatment.
- With continued drug use, frequent referral back to the same program the woman already attended.
- Few inclusions in case notes of conversations with relatives or service providers, and no accompanying notes by the supervising officer of actions in response.
- Few notes reflecting conversations, including those in which women disclosed their feelings.
- After completion of substance abuse treatment, or after a brief period of no additional illegal activity, decrease in the level of supervision, resulting in heavy use of mailed reports; or limited status from the start of supervision.
- Chronicling of problems and violations with no noted intervention.
- Chronicling of moves to new residences with no noted intervention.
- Notes about talking to women about changing their criminal thinking.

Broad and intensive tactics characterize Gender Responsive County:

- Increased level of supervision for various reasons, including little or much knowledge about women, first time or previous times under supervision, and transitioning out of a residential substance abuse treatment program.
- At least initially, little or no reliance on mailed reports and heavy reliance on frequent office appointments and unannounced home and work visits.
- Emphasis on "stabilizing housing," not allowing some moves or living arrangements.
- Coordination between the two supervising officers if the woman's current or previous partner is on probation or parole.
- Relationships with supervising officers that encourage women to disclose their feelings.
- Use of the Intensive Drug Treatment Program that included frequent drug testing and electronic surveillance, followed by aftercare treatment when the electronic surveillance was discontinued. Involvement in this program automatically and dramatically

increased treatment, since participation in both in-program treatment groups and self-help groups was required.

- Combination of the Intensive Drug Treatment Program with initial housing, sometimes for fourteen weeks, in the county work release center or jail, with gradually increasing time out of the center to search for a job, to work, and to attend self-help groups.
- Acting in response to information from family members, and communicating and coordinating with family members.
- Acting in response to disclosure of women's feelings through conversations and referrals, especially to the self-esteem, grief, and women's support groups.
- Frequent communication and coordination with personnel at substance abuse treatment, job readiness and employment, and mental health agencies.

As I previously noted, the counties' approaches are dissimilar but not completely different. For instance, references to "criminal thinking" occur much less often in Gender Responsive County than in Traditional County case notes and interview responses. Still, Gender Responsive County officers did sometimes talk about "criminal thinking," as part of a larger set of topics described in the case notes. Traditional County officers generate case notes that present only their efforts to stop "criminal thinking."

Gender Responsive County supervising officers engage in more interactions and relationships with each other and service providers. They address a much broader range of problems and life quality issues with women than the Traditional County officers do. They have many more face-to-face meetings with the women they supervise. Traditional County officers sometimes have positive relationships with women, sometimes address multiple types of problems, and may have frequent contacts and conversations with women. But even when supervision was more intense than usual in Traditional County, it could be interrupted by a transfer due to a woman's move to another zip code area, or a quick transition to limited supervision when things seemed to be going well.

In this study, the data do not support feminist concerns about stereotyping, excessive control, and punishment in the name of gender-responsive corrections. For the substance-centered women who use drugs, Gender Responsive County officers mix caring with control as they concentrate on getting women into substance abuse treatment. Many women appreciated the level of control and seemed to benefit from it. I can find no evidence that the officers stereotype women according to narrow ideas about appropriate gender roles.

Supervision practices in Traditional County obscure how well women actually fare under limited and narrow supervision. Apparent success — for example, termination of supervision — might signify only the limited nature of supervision rather than a woman's avoiding drugs and crime. By using the intensive supervision practices described in chapter 1, supervising officers can create an official record that indicates failure. Alternatively, by failing to monitor women, they can create a record of success. Thus, just as failure can be constructed through the practices of intensive supervision, success can be constructed through limited supervision.

In the next chapter, I address critical research questions about whether certain supervision tactics explain positive changes and outcomes. Did supervision produce actual positive changes? If so, how did change come about? If not, why not? To answer these questions, I look further than the official records for evidence of success. Answers to these questions may reveal additional important differences between the counties.

6

Positive Changes for
Substance-Centered Women

I became stable and [now I] think things through before
I make decisions. [It helped] to be able to talk to someone
[the supervising officer] with an objective opinion.
KELLY, Gender Responsive County

Despite long-standing, serious difficulties and limited resources, some substance-centered women did improve their lives and managed to avoid crime. I wanted to know exactly how they turned their lives around. Understanding the part that community supervision played in this process will build the knowledge base for designing effective gender-responsive programs. In this chapter, I continue to examine the lives of substance-centered women, but I focus on why drug-addicted and dependent women take steps to stop drug use and abandon criminal lifestyles.

Getting clean is the starting point for women to make other positive changes. Once women stop using drugs, they return to or find sober partners, reconnect with previously estranged law-abiding relatives, and make new friends. A Gender Responsive County mother told a supervising officer that when her daughter gave up drugs, their relationship was renewed, stating that "I really enjoy having her around now that she is not using drugs." People who previously distanced themselves from drug-using women accept them into their homes and lives once they stop using.

THE INFLUENCE OF EXTERNAL
CONTROLS AND STRUCTURE

Supervising officers and treatment program staff establish controls that prevent women from using drugs. From the women's perspective, frequent drug testing and regular appointments with the supervising officers — the norm in Gender Responsive County—promote this sort of control. Julie described how random drug testing affected her:

> I never knew when I had to come in, so I had to be ready every day. I got into the good habit of routinely calling in and being prepared. Probation gave me boundaries. Crossing that line would get me in trouble again.

Laura and Joanne, also in Gender Responsive County, made similar statements. Laura told the interviewer that random urine tests and required appointments with the supervising officer "enabled me to deal with my addiction, to face reality." Joanne said that after repeated positive tests for methamphetamine use, the Intensive Drug Treatment Program helped her the most, starting with thirty days in the work release center. She explained:

> It's kept me clean and made me organize my time better, given me tools to use that I didn't have before, and put structure back in my life, and taught organization of my time, planning, and structure.

Court-ordered intensive treatment similarly affected a Traditional County woman, who told the interviewer: "I'd be on the streets doing drugs still. I'd be dead. It's very structured. If I thought I'd get away with using I would go ahead and use. This structure kept me off of them."

THE SEQUENCE OF POSITIVE CHANGES

Along with promoting treatment and introducing controls, supervising officers hinder drug use by directing women to live in jail, the work release center, a residential treatment facility, or a new community. These living arrangements create physical distance from people who use and provide drugs.

In Gender Responsive County, supervising officers commonly force changes in women's support networks. This is accomplished by rejecting women's housing arrangements, restricting work to settings where no alcohol is served, and prohibiting association with individuals involved in crime. For example, an officer denied Kristen's request for her significant other, also a drug user, to visit her in jail. The officer told Kristen to find associates unconnected to her substance-abusing past. She also ordered her to quit her bartending job and find work at a place that did not serve alcohol. In Traditional County, officers also directed women to stay away from people who used drugs or broke the law. In fact, not associating with criminals is a typical prohibition for parolees and probationers. Despite some county similarities, Gender Responsive County case notes more often describe prohibitions against women's living arrangements, work settings, and associations. This difference results in part from Traditional County's tendency to supervise at a limited level. Limited supervision dramatically decreases attention to women's associates, work settings, and living arrangements.

Women also take their own steps to distance themselves from people who break the law. For instance, after Cheryl completed substance abuse treatment and began working full time, she told the Gender Responsive County supervising officer that when she ran into old friends who were "all strung out," it made her happy that "I did what I did [went to treatment]." She stayed away from these friends and drew support from her substance abuse treatment counselor. At the end of the year, Cheryl's support network consisted of her parents, who were not involved in illegal activity; her partner, who did not use drugs and had never been arrested; and her lawyer. Similarly Fran, another woman in Gender Responsive County, was heavily involved in both self-help group meetings and a substance abuse treatment aftercare program. Once she found these sources of support, she decided to stay out of any relationships with men so she could "work on myself and my kids."

Supervising officers' ability and means to influence positive changes in women's lives varies. Mary Anne's Gender Responsive County supervising officer initiated change by sending her to jail to stop her drug use. She promoted further change by arranging for Mary Anne to enter a residential substance abuse treatment program. The officer's case notes indicate that when Mary Anne came to pick up clothes from the officer to wear at the program site, Mary Anne "thanked me [the officer] for putting her in jail. She said she has learned a lot being there and knows now she doesn't want to live her life [the way she did] anymore." Four months later, Mary Anne completed treatment and found housing. Six months later, she found employment. Also in Gender Responsive County, Natasha initiated changes through her own motivation, combined with drug testing required by her supervising officer. She stopped using marijuana and alcohol to avoid testing positive for drug use, which she believed would cause her to lose custody of her baby, then about to be born. With support, she made several other positive changes. During the year, the supervising officer wrote that when Natasha considered moving to get away from her abusive boyfriend, the officer "reinforced GED and working." According to Natasha, this boyfriend contributed to her conviction. He "had me hold all of his drugs and the money he made from drugs, and the police arrested me for it." Natasha left him and moved to a stable and safe living situation in another county. The supervising officer in the new county noted that Natasha tried to "expand her clean and sober network" and "wants to meet more women with infants to create a new mom support network." Gender Responsive County's broad and intense supervision tactics both spark and support a series of positive changes.

Although leaving drug using and abusive men is often associated with other positive changes, it does not fully explain them. After staying in the work release center and participating in the Intensive Drug Treatment Program, Kristen found new support networks in Alcoholics Anonymous, the Gender Responsive County women's support group, and outpatient meetings at the Intensive Drug Treatment Program. Finding a decent job, learning how to keep a job, and finding a place to live preceded Kristen's leaving her drug-using partner. Getting away from this person is just one part of Kristen's lifestyle change; her supervising officer's interventions encouraged others. Kristen acted on her personal motivation to give up drugs. Finally, an accumulation of multiple resources — housing, income, and benefits from working — empowered Kristen to distance herself from people who supported drug use.

Involvement with a partner who does not commit crime or use drugs also does not fully explain shifts away from illegal behavior. New positive relationships often follow moves toward abstinence. Avoiding drugs allows women to meet drug-free people. Associating with such people in turn facilitates dating and marrying men without criminal lifestyles.

Regaining child custody can also follow other positive changes. Before returning her children, the Child and Family Services Agency required Fran to secure housing and to complete substance abuse treatment and parenting classes. Fran made a series of changes over the year, including abstaining from drugs and alcohol and attending a GED class. Legal aid helped her fight denial of housing based on her criminal history. As with many other desired outcomes, abstinence enabled women to regain custody. Fran had to meet requirements for substance abuse treatment and stable housing in order to reunite with her children.

Julie's experiences illustrate the common sequence of changes in Gender Responsive County. When Julie tested positive for methamphetamines, her supervising officer sanctioned her with sixteen hours of work crew. When her tests continued to be positive, the officer sanctioned her to an additional sixteen hours on a work crew picking up highway litter. The supervising officer helped directly and also made referrals for assistance with education, substance abuse treatment, job skills, and life skills. As a result of a referral, Julie graduated from an intense training program in computer skills, which met for twenty hours per week, for fourteen and a half weeks. After beginning outpatient substance abuse treatment, Julie regularly attended Alcoholics Anonymous. Her support network changed. Her parents consistently provided help. In addition, Julie stopped relying on a male friend, who had been arrested for drug dealing, and a female friend arrested for driving under the influence. At the end of the year, Julie told the interviewer that she relied on several new friends and her siblings without arrest records for support. She began to date a man who was not involved with crime or drugs. Julie said supervision helped because it gave her "opportunities to become more self-sufficient." Asked about the most important gain from supervision, she replied, "job skills." Julie's story demonstrates the combined effects of substance abuse treatment and job skill development in empowering women to change associates and lifestyles.

The change sequence in the two counties differs: more Gender Responsive County women attend specialized, extensive job training programs. Supervising officers required several women to contact the Employment Services Agency. That agency connected women to federally supported jobs programs, based in community colleges, to learn computer skills, warehouse management, and construction. These programs hold the promise of well-paying jobs. Although officers directed Traditional County women to work in order to pay fees, fines, and restitution, they did not push women to gain employment-related skills. Unlike the traditional supervision approach, gender-responsive supervision prepares women for jobs outside the restrictive gender-related stereotypes. Traditional County practices maintain women in the homemaker role, or in low-paying women's work.

ALTERNATIVE ROUTES TO CHANGE

In Traditional County, supervision contributes little or nothing to women's attempts to make positive changes. During interviews, several substance-centered Traditional County women explicitly separated their success in remaining in the community from their supervision. One woman described her supervision as going from a "drug PO to a regular PO to mail in." She said "family and church helped, probation didn't." In her opinion, improved supervision would be characterized by "better contact and ability to talk with the PO, not so impersonal." At the twelve-month point, Colette told the interviewer that she was in "drug rehab" before she was arrested, so her "program was established on her own." When asked about the program that helped her most, Colette instead shared her negative views of supervision: "I wished I would have done jail time instead of probation." The interviewer noted that Colette was very unhappy that "reporting had no relevance to her drug charge."

Consistent with the greater role of judges and the more limited role of supervising officers in Traditional County, a judge in that county ordered Robbie to attend the program that she found most helpful. Robbie told the interviewer that the Intensive Drug Treatment Program at the jail taught her about stress signals that indicated she should leave negative situations. The program also "allowed me to express myself and deal with it, all with people who have been in the same stuff, without worrying about hurting someone's feelings." Robbie saw no connection between the program and her supervision. She commented: "The PO didn't care that I did all I was asked to do. The PO wanted money, [and] that is all." In case notes, however, the supervising officer noted that the Intensive Drug Treatment Program would benefit Robbie. Perhaps without telling Robbie, the officer had recommended the program to the judge. It is possible that even when Traditional County officers take steps to steer women into helpful treatment, women are unaware of their actions because of the lack of communication. This is unfortunate. If women felt that supervising officers supported treatment, they might engage more in helpful conversations or other effective interventions, which often happen in Gender Responsive County.

Change Promoted by Tribal Wraparound Services

As I analyzed the data, I grew increasingly aware that substance abuse treatment and other types of help available through the local Native American tribes were accessible, intense, coordinated, and comprehensive. Tribal services met Julia's multiple and complex needs. Suffering from heart problems caused by drug use, she lived on less than $300 a month in disability payments. At the beginning of the year, she telephoned her husband's supervising officer numerous times each day to threaten her husband's life. At one point, she assaulted her husband. Then, news that she could no longer see her children triggered a drug relapse and attempted suicide. The Gender Responsive County supervising officer referred Julia to tribal substance abuse treatment services. Staff there counseled her daily, helped locate housing, and arranged mental health care. Julia told the interviewer that her support network included three women psychologists at the tribal services treatment program, and a female doctor. She described internal changes and new knowledge. She gained the ability to ask for help and information on relapse prevention and the effects of drugs on the body. She also gained self-esteem and skills to relieve stress and solve problems. Furthermore, she learned about her Native American background and related values and morals. From her standpoint, the program differed from all others she attended because of the "focus on Native American spirituality."

Julia's need for mental health treatment, suicide attempt, and violence disqualified her from most residential treatment programs for substance abuse. The tribal substance abuse treatment program, however, accepted her immediately. Staff there coordinated a variety of inpatient, outpatient, and referral services; they became Julia's support network. The program delivered culturally meaningful services. As a result, it enabled Julia to make crucial internal changes, which I discuss in detail below.

Change Promoted by Shifting to the Mental Health System

Pat, described in chapter 4, ended the year absconded; she seemed to have undiagnosed neurological problems that could not be addressed even through broad and intense supervision. In Gender Responsive County, staff also viewed Karen's needs as impossible to address in the correctional system. Her supervision started out intense and focused on substance abuse treatment. According to Karen, her supervising officer arranged appointments with a female psychiatrist and physician. In the past, mental health and physician services had refused to assign only female staff to her case, so Karen had received no treatment for severe depression. She refused to see male healthcare workers, she explained, because "I don't do well with men." Then, fairly early in her year of supervision, after she had obtained ongoing mental health services, Karen said her supervision went "from once a month to nothing." This quick drop in supervision is unusual in Gender Responsive County.

Karen's diagnosis of severe depression and her reports to the interviewer of the effectiveness of medication indicate that the officer's efforts to give her access to treatment resulted in positive change. Yet, like Pat, Karen's problems stemmed primarily from mental illness. The supervising officer wrote: "Mental health issues may make cognitive programming inappropriate." Unlike Pat, Karen did not abscond. However, the supervising officer shifted intervention from community corrections to the mental health system. At the year-end interview, Karen included the mental health workers in her support network. The justice system acted primarily and appropriately to connect Karen with mental health services and shift her out of the correctional system.

PERSISTENT BARRIERS TO SUBSTANCE ABUSE TREATMENT

As shown in several examples from Gender Responsive County, active drug users experiencing some success confront obstacles to accessing treatment just as often as the women who failed, described in chapter 5. Mary Anne spent time in jail waiting for space in residential treatment facilities. Mary waited for space there, too, but lived in the community. Betty regularly shot up heroin while waiting for admission to the methadone maintenance program. She told the officer she was "trying to hold on until I get on methadone." Cheryl stayed in the community, too, but could not begin treatment because her insurance did not cover the outpatient program that had openings. Judy secured a space in the recommended residential program, but immediately after graduation, she had no place to live. Serendipitously, the program just then opened transitional housing, which the counselor indicated would "give her a chance to get rental credit, get a job, and get on her feet." Despite obstacles to services, generally the strenuous efforts of supervising officers led to eventual treatment or suitable housing for all of these women.

Especially in Gender Responsive County, supervising officers who have ongoing relationships and contacts with women fill in gaps in service by arranging for alternative temporary substance abuse treatment or by directly meeting needs themselves. They administer drug tests and refer women to outpatient treatment until residential treatment opens up. Women's heavy use of dangerous combinations of drugs and their physical symptoms — like visible sores, a burst blood vessel in the eye, and needle marks — lead officers to jail women until programs can accept them. Finally, when women lack other support, Gender Responsive County supervising officers increase conversations and visits with the women.

CHANGES IN THE SELF

In the previous chapter, I described a few women who experienced internal changes that seemed to support abstinence from drugs. Particularly in Gender Responsive County, several substance-centered women commented to interviewers about such changes in their feelings, thoughts, and perceptions.

Women attributed internal changes to positive relationships with the Gender Responsive County officers. They also said that participation in special groups, counseling, and substance abuse treatment led to positive internal changes. They described changes such as new learning and recognition, including seeing themselves "in a new light" (Fran), "finding myself" (Cheryl), and gaining a sense of support and of not being alone. Kelly, whose comment opens this chapter, believed that conversations with the supervising officer improved her decision-making ability. Women explicitly connect internal changes to supervising officers' attention and helpful responses to their feelings.

Regardless of the county, substance abuse treatment programs also help women see themselves more positively and as not alone. They teach women to solve problems. More specifically, they teach them to beat addiction by recognizing the circumstances and feelings that trigger drug use. Alexandra, from Traditional County, summarized many reasons for change. She explained that the substance abuse treatment program she attended "made me aware of what I need to do to get what I want. The drugs — they [staff in the program] teach you ways to say no and setting up boundaries, and learning to be me." She especially liked "the way the group makes me feel, like part of the herd. We are all the same. It makes me feel good inside because I'm trusted in the group." The program differed from others she attended because "the counselors care more about our feelings and needs here. They listen better. They won't judge me. They are able to see right away how important my needs are."

In Gender Responsive County, women point to the critical impact of woman-only groups on positive internal changes. Betty said the most helpful program provided a "caring, loving environment . . . due to the fact that only women are here. Men [in programs] cause distractions and too much competition between women." In a similar vein, Kristen said that the substance abuse treatment built her self-esteem and sense of self-worth because of "the honesty and that I was able to talk to the other women in the program."

Women who fail programs by breaking rules or not meeting requirements experience gaps in treatment until they start a new program. Ongoing conversations with supervising officers and participating in Gender Responsive County's special groups fill the gaps. The site of internal change in Gender Responsive County is more often within the special groups and in interaction with supervising officers. For Traditional County women, internal change occurs more exclusively in treatment programs.

THE JUSTICE OF EXTREME CONTROL

Gender Responsive County supervising officers manage women's relapses and act aggressively to control drug use. They exert their powers through actions as well as conversations with the women, their relatives, and other service providers. Supervision exposes and addresses many facets of women's lives. As I highlight in the introduction, feminist researchers raise concerns that intense monitoring and programming increases controls on women unjustly, with no benefit.

I examined Joanne's high-level supervision to see whether controls had unreasonably restricted her freedom. At first, Joanne seemed to have many resources and limited problems. She had finished three years of college, earned $3,000 to $4,000 a month at a full-time job, received child-support payments for her teenage son, and lived free of charge with her parents. From the start, her support network consisted of several family members with no arrest history. Joanne staged her own robbery at the restaurant where she worked. Her employer fired her, but she immediately found another job. Within the year, she found an even better job. Despite Joanne's many advantages, intensive supervision, which included drug testing, revealed a history of substance abuse going back to her teen years. At the age of thirty, she regularly used methamphetamines. The Gender Responsive County's sudden-strike style of supervision quickly resulted in Joanne's living in the work release center and attending the Intensive Drug Treatment Program. I do not know whether less oversight or milder intervention would have led to the positive outcome that Joanne attributed to the intensive treatment. In any case, Joanne believed that supervision got her "off drugs." Some women expressed ambivalence about the Gender Responsive County's supervision style. A few were consistently negative. However, the majority of the women were positive and appreciated even intrusive and controlling supervision.

QUESTIONS ABOUT THE STABILITY
OF POSITIVE CHANGE

Active drug users who experienced some success ended the year with remaining challenges. Relationships with children were especially problematic. Some women felt grief and anger over permanent loss of child custody, even if this had occurred many years earlier. At the worst, women talked about relapsing as a result of the temporary or permanent loss of their children. They also grieved over past abortions. Some tried to keep or regain child custody, but due to drug relapses and dangerous, inadequate residences, their children almost always remained dispersed among foster parents, their fathers, or other relatives. A few women had a child with them at some point during the year, or had the hope of regaining custody. Regaining child custody posed its own challenges, since many women had children with emotional or physical problems.

The serious nature of remaining problems and the women's long histories of drug use led me to question the stability of any positive changes. Were breaks from taking drugs and active participation in treatment enough to ensure that women would not relapse and break the law again? What would happen when external controls ended?

I answer these questions in the next chapter, which focuses on substance-centered women who stopped using drugs before supervision began. The chapter concentrates on the combination of women's actions and circumstances, and the supervision tactics that produce continued cessation of substance abuse. The chapter provides a further test of the effectiveness of gender-responsive tactics that, so far, seem to lead to positive outcomes.

7

Keeping Women off Drugs

Drugs have a power over me when I use them.
Drugs is all I ever did, but now I am clean.
JEN, Gender Responsive County

As Jen recognizes, a new life depends on stopping drug use. Despite obstacles, some women driven by personal motivations maintain drug-free lifestyles throughout the year of supervision. Gender-responsive supervision tactics help prevent relapse by promoting positive changes that reduce the pressure on women to use drugs.

Nearly half of substance-centered women who started the year abstinent in Traditional County received the most minimal level of monitoring and supervision. Drug tests were scheduled less than monthly, or not at all. Women often did not report in person or even by mail. The only program they attended provided HIV/AIDS education.

Even for drug-abstinent women, Gender Responsive County supervising officers made numerous home visits and referrals, and pushed other programs to deliver needed services. After a period of high contact, officers reduced supervision levels over the course of the year, but not as quickly or as much as Traditional County officers. In Gender Responsive County, only Barb experienced limited and narrow supervision. Atypically, her supervising officer changed three times. The final officer, who retired, encouraged Barb to attend the self-esteem group, a source of ongoing support. Because of this group, Barb received more correctional programming than most Traditional County women.

In the previous chapter, I questioned whether even intense and broad supervision suffices to promote abstinence and keep women crime free. Do the effective gender-responsive tactics discovered thus far maintain abstinence for extended periods? Does something other than Traditional County supervision explain the apparent success of those women who abstained all year? I wanted to know whether supervision strategies that promoted women's abstinence could effectively prevent relapse for a full year. A finding of continued effectiveness would strengthen my belief in the utility of Gender Responsive County's supervision practices. I also wanted to understand how some Traditional County women managed to finish the year successfully, despite limited supervision.

In total, fifty-one substance-centered women who began supervision were already abstinent from drugs. Twenty-two were in Gender Responsive County, and twenty-nine in Traditional County. In both counties, this group makes up 20 percent of the substance-centered women.

TRADITIONAL COUNTY'S LIMITED
ATTENTION TO WOMEN'S NEEDS

At first, Victoria's Traditional County supervising officer addressed the same range of needs and encouraged the same immersion in services that characterizes Gender Responsive County. At the beginning of supervision, case notes document that Victoria had just left an inpatient substance abuse treatment center and was living in transitional housing. She wanted to regain custody of two children in foster care. Her husband had sole custody of their third child. The supervising officer provided help and referrals in a range of areas: health care, HIV/AIDS education, job skills, child custody, housing, life skills, and parenting. However, several new problems arose during the year. The transitional housing program evicted Victoria for nonpayment of back rent. In addition, Victoria quit her job, she said, because too many employees used drugs. Her six-year-old also began acting out sexually, due to prior sexual abuse. After foster parents indicated they could not handle him, the Child and Family Services Agency moved up the schedule for Victoria's children to return to her custory. Victoria missed the deadline for reapplying for state medical insurance, so she lost the means to pay for substance abuse aftercare. At this point, the supervising officer reduced supervision to a low level. Shortly after Victoria completed aftercare treatment, the officer ended contact by moving her to limited supervision. This pattern stands in sharp contrast to that of Gender Responsive County, where escalating problems are typically met with escalating supervision. In Traditional County, if women meet court-ordered requirements, supervision decreases regardless of whether the women's needs are proliferating. Yet Victoria ended the year without using drugs, with a new job and custody of her children, and participating in Alcoholics Anonymous. Success does not always require intense supervision throughout the year.

There is evidence, though, that the Traditional County approach leaves women with unmet needs that may lead to renewed drug use or other criminal behavior. Consistent with the quick shift to minimal supervision, a Traditional County officer indicated in the research survey that Dian "was an excellent probationer, reported as directed, completed all conditions promptly, and was rewarded with bench probation." Dian presented a very different picture:

> They haven't done anything for me. All I've done is stress out about getting that report done by the first [mailing her report to the supervising officer by the first of each month] and having the $35 [supervision fee]. Supervision hasn't helped at all—going to jail, losing kids and home cured me. The PO didn't return calls. I learned nothing. [The supervising officer should] help more with job training. Being a convicted felon made it extremely hard, especially with no skills.

Dian's children moved from foster care to her parents' home, and she hoped to eventually regain custody. Working as a part-time waitress, she earned $5.50 an hour. Aside from avoiding drug use and illegal activity, Dian made no other positive changes. Her circumstances signal a high likelihood of future problems.

In another Traditional County example, Rene's supervising officer chronicled but did not intervene in her problems. Police initially believed she lived in a drug house, but later determined it was a "former drug house." Her conviction disqualified her for training as a real-estate appraiser, a job with high potential for a good income. Rene told the interviewer that throughout the year, her partner had hurt and bruised her "once a month or more." Rene described her supervision to the interviewer, and the interviewer asked questions to obtain more details:

> It was nothing. It was mail-in reporting. [Interviewer: "What was good about it?"] There was no effort, just mailing, and I didn't have to think about it, trouble, and the law all the time. [Interviewer: "What didn't you like?"] Feeling like a number, [the supervising officer] not seeing I'm a

person. [Interviewer: "How could it be improved?"] Caring about me in the first place — finding out why this all happened.

Rene ended the year living with the same abusive partner who had contributed to her conviction by forcing her to cash bad checks. She depended on him for living expenses because her pay as a motel maid was so low. Despite her official "success" on supervision, Rene recognized the precariousness of her situation and her need for more help.

QUESTIONABLE EVIDENCE THAT
LIMITED SUPERVISION WORKS

As I found for other subgroups of women, in Traditional County, programs and resources that were unconnected to supervision influenced abstinence and positive change. A mental health program referred Flo to a group for adults who had been molested as children. That program, not supervision, made a considerable difference to her, because it addressed her long-standing problems with severe depression. Flo said: "What makes it a good group is being believed and encouraged but not forced to talk about your feelings." She described the counselor as "very understanding and loving." She compared the group to a different one in prison, which had struck her as "artificial and not compassionate. It stirred up feelings that couldn't be addressed in that atmosphere." Tribal resources provided substantial help in both counties. In Traditional County, an annual stipend from the tribe enabled one woman to begin paying $3,000 in court costs. After she lost her job due to the felony conviction, the tribe hired her to work at a casino and paid her $400 a month during the training period.

Limited supervision in Traditional County did not match the magnitude of abstinent women's troubles. An officer's notes describe Anne's serious history of drug abuse. Anne had injected heroin daily for three years, and her sister died from a heroin overdose a year before Anne's supervision started. Yet Anne never attended substance abuse treatment. After she failed to mail in reports for five months, the officer directed her to pay fees and obtain a substance abuse evaluation. Neither case notes nor the interview responses document any evaluation or treatment during the year. In the twelfth month of supervision, the officer put Anne on the most limited supervision because of her low-risk status. Anne said of the experience: "I wasn't really supervised. I only saw the PO once." The interviewer summed up her own impressions:

> She was able to help herself. She had a strong enough will to change herself. Her PO never asked the important questions like if she was using and why. Her mother really helped her to open her eyes to see what real friends are and cold, hard facts about users.

Women's own determination, together with pressure from people who were not a part of community supervision, most affected the success of abstinent Traditional County women.

SUPERVISION THAT KEEPS WOMEN OFF DRUGS

Based on her background, I would not be surprised if Pam spent the study year on the streets and addicted. She first used cocaine, pills, marijuana, and LSD at age thirteen. As a result of sexual abuse by her mother's boyfriend, Pam gave birth to a daughter at age sixteen. The police first arrested her for prostitution as a teenager. Several arrests followed for burglary, assault, and possession, delivery, and manufacture of a controlled substance. At the outset of supervision, Pam lived with an abusive, drug-using partner in a jointly owned house. She wanted to leave, but she delayed until they could prepare the property to sell it. She planned to use the sale proceeds to purchase a home suitable for keeping, raising, and selling pet animals. Pam told the supervising officer her partner's drug use in the house made her want to use, but she worked hard to stay clean. At one point, out of anger, she broke her partner's dope pipe. He tried to choke her, and she called the police, who refused to arrest him. She decided not to call the police again, since that could jeopardize her partner's paying for home improvements needed to sell the house. When a medical condition kept her from her regular job, she earned money from selling pet animals and cosmetics. When the house eventually sold, she moved. Despite the odds against her, Pam finished the year without using drugs.

The nature of Pam's supervision shows the impact of broad and intense intervention for the group considered in this chapter. Pam explained:

> [Supervision gives] an outlook on what your life is about. You analyze it and it gives you some thoughts. The PO is wonderful. Once we decided

to respect each other, we can now have a really good conversation. I know she is behind me no matter what decision I make. She is one of the best POs there. But if I messed up, she would throw me back in jail. I like least that I cannot fool the PO, cannot play games. They [probation and parole staff] are all over everything. I can't get away with anything, but I guess I shouldn't try to do that anyway.

The supervising officer referred Pam to drug and mental health treatment, and talked with her at length during frequent office and home visits. She carried out at least one home visit jointly with the supervising officer for Pam's partner. She changed Pam's deadline for completing treatment, to allow Pam to address medical problems and continue working. Improved physical health and continued earnings enabled Pam to leave her partner.

Pam invested her own time and money to avoid drugs. She saved $225 to pay for a substance abuse evaluation, and later lived in the work release center while successfully completing the Intensive Drug Treatment Program. She paid her supervision fees and cooperated in drug testing. Near the end of the year, Pam read a newspaper ad for a drug education program at a local university; on her own, she registered and attended. She described the program as helpful because it built self-esteem. She appreciated that in the program "you get feedback for talking about problems" and "you talk to people about problems confidentially."

Pam's experience confirms the benefit of several Gender Responsive County supervision tactics. Supervision contributed to Pam's efforts to leave her partner, alter her lifestyle, and change her support network. These improvements empowered Pam to attend the university support group, which produced additional positive changes.

Comprehensive Attention to Needs

When women stop using drugs, officers no longer need to spend inordinate amounts of time struggling with them over starting treatment. Though they still monitor drug use, officers can focus on a greater range of issues. Services become increasingly comprehensive and may continue throughout the year of supervision and beyond.

Concrete assistance remains a unique key feature of Gender Responsive County supervision, even after women stop using drugs. Supervising officers provide sanitary pads, shampoo, toothpaste, and hair conditioner.

One officer helped Danny, afflicted with brain damage due to domestic violence and drug use, get clothes and furniture as well as a decent place to live. When appropriate, Gender Responsive County officers made referrals to a federal program that provides health care, nutritious food, and pregnancy and parenting education. A woman who received concrete help said: "My PO is a great support, especially because she knows where to get help if I needed help. My PO gave me security by being there for me."

In addition to concrete assistance, supervision focuses on an increasing array of issues over the year, even when women have stopped using drugs. This pattern characterizes Kristy's gender-responsive supervision. A referral to the Employment Services Agency started a chain of events that allowed her to enroll in a training program for construction supply specialists. In addition to this community college program, which met more than twenty hours each week for eighteen weeks, the supervising officer also sent Kristy to an alcohol and drug support group. Kristy said this group gave her a "drug-free lifestyle, love of self, better parenting skills, a role model [the counselor], and a support system to turn to for help." Reflecting the positive relationship, Kristy told the interviewer: "I love my PO and think she is a great, helpful person." To increase the chance of regaining child custody, Kristy attended Narcotics Anonymous meetings. The benefits for her included "people to look up to. It's been there longer than me. [I like] the bond that you get with people." During the year, she married a man who contributed to their household income and had no drug or criminal history. Ending drug use made the other positive changes possible. Kristy's motivations, choices, and actions combined with multiple sources of support based on her strong connection to her supervising officer led to positive change.

Gender Responsive County supervising officers continuously reevaluate women's specific needs and then rematch them to appropriate services and groups. As a result, women receive multiple services simultaneously or in succession. Alice attended a succession of groups. The supervising officer referred her to a program for women who had been prostitutes. Alice said the "therapist was sincere, wonderful. She helped me most in a personal way, helped me believe in myself. [She taught me] how to keep your chin up when everybody's talking you down." Alice went on to say that "friendship" would make the program even better: "I was looking for a friend." To some extent, the supervising officer filled the vacuum; Alice commented that compared to earlier supervision experiences, this time she was "more intimate with the PO." Later in the year, Alice did find friends in the self-esteem group:

> It was a wonderful program. It made me feel like I belonged there. I could relate with everybody in the group. It made me feel like a person. I always walked out from the meeting in a positive way. [Skills were] how to handle other people. The other ones [programs] did not give me the tools on how to deal with my problems.

Over the year, in addition to developing a positive relationship with Alice, the supervising officer helped and made referrals for Alice in the areas of education, learning problems, substance abuse, mental health, domestic violence, general health, and job skills.

Like other substance-centered women who found some success, members of the abstaining group experienced positive internal change. After finishing substance abuse treatment, Mandy lived with her husband, and they regained child custody. Even though Mandy's husband worked, the officer referred Mandy to the Employment Services Agency. With the employment counselor's support, Mandy finished her GED, and the agency paid for the family's car insurance. The Employment Services Agency connected her to a community college training program, which, she said, "helped my self-esteem, preparing me for a job and a way to get advanced schooling, gave me a sense of purpose and makes me happy." Compared to other programs, it was "much more encouraging and had more one-on-one attention, no put downs." Gender-responsive supervision opened up multiple chances to succeed, which then connected Mandy to other opportunities. Comprehensive attention to her goals and needs helped Mandy feel more whole and complete as a person.

Lengthy, high-level supervision in Gender Responsive County increases communication with supervising officers. Shared information sparks concern about relapse and steps up efforts to prevent drug use. In sharp contrast, the push toward less and less supervision in Traditional County leaves supervising officers unaware of women's needs and problems.

Improving Support Networks

The Gender Responsive County special groups — like self-esteem groups and women's support groups — provide essential support for women after they stop using drugs. The groups connect women in similar circumstances. As one Gender Responsive County woman put it, groups helped by giving her a place to "listen to more people talk about their problems." Asked about the most helpful programming, another replied: "being [in the group] with other women who are also on probation, [so] I don't feel so bad about myself anymore. I always thought I was a bad person for getting into trouble with the law, and the women in my group are nice, respectful people." A small proportion of Traditional County women found similar support in treatment programs. In supportive groups, similarly situated women help each other by contradicting assumptions that offenders are "all bad" and by showing women they are not alone. Women can attend the special Gender Responsive County groups frequently and continuously, which prevents gaps in the continuity of support — for instance, when substance abuse treatment ends.

Given the backgrounds of substance-centered women, I would expect them to have extremely powerful, negative, and complex feelings. Treatment and counseling groups equip women to deal with negative feelings like grief, stress, and anger. As Flo, on the Traditional County caseload, said about her therapy in a mental health group, it helped to "get the shit out." Tina stated that a required Gender Responsive County drug treatment group "taught me to stop using drugs and live without needing those things. I could express myself freely and get any input I needed. I learned about my emotions, how to understand my emotions."

Holly, a participant in the Gender Responsive County self-esteem group, explained that it changed how she saw and thought about things: "It gave me the tools to deal with other people, and made me aware of what to watch for, to be honest with myself and to think things through. It gave me time to take care of myself and taught me to be a better parent." Having a support group helped Holly resist her drug-involved husband's attempts to get back together. Even when he moved from another state to join her, she maintained a separate residence with her children. When her substance abuse counseling ended, Holly continued with the self-esteem group.

Gender Responsive County women, who attended groups most often, derived the greatest benefit from relationships with group leaders. One said: "The instructor cared about me and has a sense of humor." Another liked her substance abuse counselor's "personal interest in patients," and the fact that "she always has time to address immediate concerns." The few criticisms of groups connected to supervision and treatment had to do with lack of structure and sufficient time for all participants to talk.

Because of numerous referrals and requirements to obtain help, Gender Responsive County women often add professionals such as lawyers and psychologists to their support networks. When her criminally involved husband moved into the area, Holly turned not only to the self-esteem group for support, but also relied on her social worker. Women drew support from professionals who were "like friends," counselors who were former addicts that the women could "relate to" and other women who participated in groups. The women turned to Alcoholics, Narcotics, and Gamblers Anonymous as alternative or additional groups.

Joan's supervision was atypically high for Traditional County, because of her record of violence. Her comments provide a good example of effective group support through a unique Narcotics Anonymous (NA) program:

> There were social activities. Good friendships are created there. It helps me stay clean and sober through networks of support. Other NA programs are very structured and are in buildings where there are lots of other groups using the facilities. This is an actual house whose sole purpose is for NA activities, support, and socializing.

Asked what would make the program even better, Joan mentioned "more women's meetings and more meetings scheduled in general." This qualification regarding programming echoes previous examples of the belief of Traditional County women that they receive less help than they need. In Gender Responsive County, supervising officers would require women like Joan to attend multiple support groups.

Improving Job Opportunities

More lengthy supervision and the ties between community corrections and the Employment Services Agency enabled several drug-free Gender Responsive County women to access quite promising employment counseling, training, and placement. To illustrate, Sherry started out making only $50 a week caring for her ailing father. The supervising officer referred her to the Employment Services Agency, which helped her prepare and type a résumé and taught her job interview skills. The agency paid for reading glasses, which she needed to work. As a result, Sherry obtained her highest paying job ever, making $300 a week. When women in Gender Responsive County work at or apply to very low paying jobs, for example as hotel maids or part-time caretakers for the sick and elderly, officers require them to go to the Employment Services Agency to obtain better jobs.

In Traditional County, the abrupt termination of supervision once conditions are met limits referrals for job training. By the middle of the year, Autumn had completed substance abuse treatment and had a new boyfriend and newborn baby. After the court denied a request to terminate her supervision, the officer transferred her to low supervision and later to the limited supervision caseload. Case notes describe Autumn at the end of the year as "now unemployed and acting as a homemaker for employed husband." Traditional County accepts dead-end, low-paying jobs and dependence on partners. Gender Responsive County promotes women's self-sufficiency through stable, decent-paying jobs. The philosophy in Gender Responsive County challenges the stereotype of women as dependent, which plays out in officers' emphasis on self-sufficiency.

The focus on work and training rebuts concerns that gender-responsive supervision reproduces narrow gender roles. In fact, by promoting "the stand-alone woman," Gender Responsive County officers enhance independence. Officers respond to dependence on abusive or lawbreaking partners by helping women obtain the resources needed to end such relationships; they also advise or may even order women to end destructive relationships.

I first encountered this notion of the "stand alone woman" in research on how correctional practitioners view effective management and programming for women offenders (Morash and Robinson 2002). One prison warden described an effective program: "The program seeks to develop stand alone women, [and] tries to make the women understand they do not need to live in a relationship that is not beneficial to them and helps them recognize and avoid codependency" (104).

Encouraging and developing stand-alone women goes beyond addressing personal problems. It empowers women by improving their social location. Women who obtain training for good jobs not only cover living expenses, but also receive benefits like medical, vision, and dental coverage for themselves and their children. They may acquire noncriminal coworkers, who can be friends, advisors, and roommates. As one feminist scholar puts it, effective programs empower women by addressing their dependent status (Belknap 1996, 107).

DEGREES OF DIFFERENCE

In my analysis of women who continued to use drugs (see chapters 5 and 6), I found clear but not absolute county differences. This pattern holds true for abstinent women. In a deviation from the norm, a Gender Responsive County woman described disorganized and poorly structured aftercare following residential treatment. Her supervising officer changed "without notice," and supervision "didn't offer needed programming. I did everything on my own." In an atypical instance in Traditional County, one woman told the interviewer that supervision helped "me keep in line, off the drugs, and the support I got was incredible. There was good, open communication with the PO." County differences, however, outnumber the similarities.

I showed in previous chapters that Gender Responsive County supervision pressures women to stop using drugs. In this chapter, I provide evidence that abstinence enables women to find and keep employment, regain child custody, and participate in training and education programs. Yet many still need help from supervising officers or others. Women split their energies between meeting key priorities, such as fulfilling community service requirements, bonding with children, dealing with custody issues, and earning a living. Gender Responsive County practices create ties between women and ongoing support networks that are available both inside and outside supervision. Those on the outside remain available even after supervision ends. These support networks give women considerable access to resources, emotional help, and companionship. Gender Responsive County further empowers women through an emphasis on good jobs.

In the next chapter, I examine how gender-responsive supervision tactics empower women in subgroups not categorized as substance-centered. The chapter compares county practices and outcomes for women in several different subgroups.

8

Supervision for Women without Drug Problems

[Gender Responsive County officers] were more concerned with me and not just the paying of restitution on time. They are sincerely interested in how I am doing.

MICHELLE, Gender Responsive County

As Michelle indicates, Gender Responsive County uses a needs-based, intensive supervision approach for at least some women who are not substance-centered. This chapter addresses the questions: Do differences by county exist for all subgroups? Does the supervision style in both counties depend on the nature of the women's crimes? What is the outcome for women? To answer these questions, I consider each of the subgroups in turn. I order the subgroups according to their similarity to substance-centered women. The first subgroups, violence-involved and partner-influenced women, are most similar in background to substance-centered women. Two other subgroups, economic offenders and marijuana cultivators, differ considerably from the others, notably in terms of their fewer problems and greater resources.

WOMEN CONVICTED OF VIOLENT ACTS

In both counties, supervising officers usually require women to participate in groups to address violence issues. Following policy, officers start out supervision of all violence-involved women at a high level. However, gender-responsive officers connect women to a greater variety of programs and a broader range of groups.

Comparing the experiences of two women illustrates how the counties differ. Both women had belonged to violent groups. Deborah spent several years in prison after she and her associates killed a child. In prison, Deborah completed her GED, a career development workshop, college classes, and several mental health and treatment groups. Her Gender Responsive County supervision focused on explaining and enforcing prohibitions against being with children; attending the self-esteem group; and referrals for health care, jobs, housing, and life skills. In Traditional County, Cassandra's supervising officer prohibited her from associating with gang members, who had contributed to her violence. Cassandra told the interviewer the required anger management group "helped me to control my anger better, know when to walk away, see the signals when I start to get mad, see things from both sides." The Gender Responsive County self-esteem group had a broader focus than the anger management group that Cassandra attended. Also, the Gender Responsive County officer addressed a broader set of needs.

Two of the nine violence-involved women from Traditional County, and none of the four from Gender Responsive County, were arrested during the year. I can draw only limited conclusions from this finding because the numbers are so small. However, Gender Responsive County's concrete help, positive relationships with officers, special groups, and wraparound services may limit new offenses for violence-involved women.

WOMEN INFLUENCED BY THEIR PARTNERS

The six partner-influenced women are divided equally between counties. The women's criminal cases were aiding, abetting, and — as the women described it — "helping" and "taking the rap for" their partners. All partner-influenced women ended the year living in the community without new arrests. The three in Gender Responsive County left the men who contributed to their crimes, while the three in Traditional County did not. Supervision tactics account for the difference.

In the case notes, the Gender Responsive County supervising officers justified high-level supervision by citing the serious needs of the three women. Jean, for example, had numerous needs and problems: a verified medical disability, which prevented her from working; status as a single parent of three teenagers, one of whom abused Jean and the other children; chronic pain and health problems that required several medications; and continued abuse by her ex-husband. In addition to requiring Jean to complete community service work, the officer addressed mental health, job skills, and intimate partner abuse issues. Jean told the interviewer that required frequent meetings with the officer helped "because my PO takes the time to talk to us. She is one of a kind. I have a PO who understands and helps me make better choices." In her view, supervision taught her "how to cope with stress and have better judgment. It opened my eyes, that my daughter needs me." She learned to "select my company and be more aware of people, keep my eyes open regarding others, and change social networks." After leaving her partner, Jean said: "I am basically alone now [but I have] less chances of getting into trouble."

Similarly, the Gender Responsive County officer helped Kimberly leave an abusive partner. Kimberly's most recent convictions were for driving her husband to a department store so he could rob a woman, and for check forging. Her husband insisted that she commit these crimes so he would have money to buy drugs. The officer wrote that Kimberly's "past crimes and convictions were all men-related, such as aiding and abetting. She needs assertiveness skills badly." In addition to coaching Kimberly in assertiveness skills, the supervising officer advised Kimberly to end financial reliance on her abusive husband and new boyfriend by finding a full-time job. She also referred her to domestic violence counseling, the self-esteem group, and a class on stress management. After Kimberly found a job, she told the officer she owned only one dress. The officer "put the word out" for donated clothing. When Kimberly lost her job and moved in with a man she hardly knew, the officer uncovered the man's prior charge for sexual assault. On advice from the officer, Kimberly transferred to another county to live with her mother. Kimberly told the interviewer that, through the self-esteem group and probation, "I learned to stand up for myself and I do not have to take men's crap." She liked "getting together with all women who are having similar problems." Financial independence and growing assertiveness enable Gender Responsive County women to leave the men who had influenced them to break the law.

Traditional County supervision does not routinely address women's attachment to crime-promoting men. Annette told the interviewer that she still lived with the man who "had meth and pot in the house, and is the reason for my legal problems today." She described him as a "very important" individual in her support network. In explaining Traditional County supervision, she stated: "They haven't really done anything. I was a pretty law-abiding person before and still am. It's been so minimal there is nothing to like or dislike." Annette said supervision would have helped her more if "they had shown more concern for me as a person, not just a statistic."

Sally's Traditional County supervising officer noted providing some direct help, but no referrals for domestic violence, pregnancy care and education, and parenting skills. Sally ignored these topics when the interviewer asked about the most helpful program. Instead, she identified the one-day court-ordered defensive driving class. Apparently, the court required her to attend the class because, during a police pursuit, she moved from the passenger side to the driver's seat to "take the rap" for her live-in partner. Sally said the driving class taught her awareness "of other drivers and what they're doing." This is an extreme example of a mismatch between the causes of lawbreaking and probation intervention. Sally's poor skills in defensive driving did not contribute to her arrest. Clearly, counseling and referrals to empower Sally to leave her partner would have been much more effective.

WOMEN CONVICTED OF CHILD MALTREATMENT

Quite a few women convicted solely for child maltreatment viewed their charges, convictions, and supervision as uncalled for and unjust. In Gender Responsive County, the Child and Family Services Agency placed one woman's three children in foster care due to unclean and substandard housing. The woman told the interviewer:

[Supervision] has nothing to do with my individual needs and legal situation. I'm a very busy person and it's difficult to add another appointment into the schedule. I should have just been put on mail-in reporting.

Two Traditional County women expressed similar frustration. According to the officer, one could not understand why she was charged with neglect after police found her child at a drug raid. The other saw no reason for justice system involvement, since a baby-sitter, not she, had hit her child.

In both counties, community supervision and Child and Family Services Agency requirements substantially overlap. Both agencies direct women to attend parenting and anger management classes. All women in the child maltreatment subgroup ended the year successfully reunited with their children.

REPEAT ECONOMIC OFFENDERS

If their problems were limited, regardless of the county, economic offenders received relatively limited supervision. Supervising officers and judges routinely referred women to private contractors, who delivered group programming designed to develop insight into the causes and consequences of property crime. The officers responded to slips with minimal sanctions. For example, Helene embezzled the substantial amount of $50,000 after a few months of supervision; in response, the Gender Responsive County officer sanctioned her with thirty days in the work release center. In Traditional County, a repeat economic offender's new conviction for forgery resulted in ten days in jail and an extended probation period. Officers did not issue progressively more severe warnings or order community service or longer jail stays, as they did for substance-centered women. They tested few of the women for drugs, and they stopped testing after a few negative results.

Although supervision is generally less intense for economic offenders than for substance-centered women, Gender Responsive County officers engaged in more office and home visits and required more group and individual counseling sessions. The officers justified intervention with comments like, "She is a theft client who needs to be supervised at a medium level until counseling is set up," and "This is a second-time embezzler who needs closer supervision because of job changes." Supervision in Gender Responsive County entailed participation in a special program for women embezzlers, the self-esteem group, and a penitentiary tour. In one case, additional counseling was required to address what the officer described as a dysfunctional relationship with an intimate partner who promoted the economic crime. As I found for substance-centered women, county differences are pronounced but not absolute.

The following examples illustrate the greater supervision found in Gender Responsive County. Elizabeth, a repeat economic offender, described heavy monitoring: "I had to report personal details to the PO. I felt a loss of control over my life." Most other women valued the officers' help and attention. Michelle said the sex abuse survivor group "helped me on my communication. I now talk to people about things and what is going on. That, I would not have done before." As quoted at the beginning of the chapter, she compared Gender Responsive County officers to those in another county: "They were more concerned with me and not just the paying of restitution on time. They are sincerely interested in how I am doing." Whitney believed her supervision in Gender Responsive County was unstructured but helpful. She said "it helped me think more openly about the real reasons I embezzled. Hearing other women's experiences made me feel less singled out." She learned to "keep an open mind on the big picture and think about things in a different perspective." Like substance-centered women, many repeat economic offenders appreciated gender-responsive supervision because it addressed their particular needs.

Greater assistance in Gender Responsive County helped some women change the circumstances that contributed to their economic offenses. While unemployed, Cheri stole almost $4,000 from her mother. Initially, she lived with her alcoholic boyfriend and their infant. When he threatened their child, she moved in with her husband. After discovering drugs in her husband's trailer, she moved out. The officer counseled Cheri to avoid both of these men and to obtain training and eventual employment. Cheri explained that supervision helped her more than any program by showing "what I need to do to take care of myself and my daughter." By the end of the year, as a result of a referral from the supervising officer, Cheri had enrolled in a community college program to develop computer skills.

Not all repeat economic offenders avoid crime. Some continue to steal or fraudulently collect public benefits. Others end the year successful, but less as a result of supervision than of changing life circumstances — for example, a father who begins to support the family after a child is born. On average, though, compared to the Traditional County hands-off approach, needs-based supervision in Gender Responsive County promotes more positive change and less illegal behavior for this group.

ONE-TIME ECONOMIC OFFENDERS

Women in the one-time economic offender group (and in the marijuana cultivator group, discussed next) differ from most others. As discussed in chapter 3, they often live in intact nuclear families with children and spouses, with law-abiding partners, or with parents. Many have been married for years. They usually hold high-school degrees, and several have attended college. Women in the one-time offender group did not break the law again during the year.

Several one-time economic offenders felt their sentences and supervision were undeserved. They told interviewers things like:

> I don't think it was necessary for us to be on supervision. I don't have a drug problem but I have good fair values. (Gender Responsive County)
>
> [Interviewer: "What changes would you recommend in supervision?"] No changes. I just want off of it. I have never been in any trouble before. There are many people in much worse trouble that could use it. (Gender Responsive County)
>
> The justice system is awful. It is too drug-oriented. Not everyone has drug issues. (Gender Responsive County)

Some one-time economic offenders defend themselves as people who do not "make it a habit to break laws" and resent justice system interventions. Others are upset or remorseful about criminal acts that they view as uncharacteristic. All of them see themselves as essentially law-abiding.

Nonetheless, Gender Responsive County officers routinely require these women to attend "theft talks," to complete "penitentiary tours," and to participate in special groups. Officers justify more supervision than indicated by the women's risk scores, citing reasons such as lack of remorse, suspected domestic violence, failure to meet conditions of supervision in a timely manner, and unmet needs.

Linda's supervising officer, for example, felt she needed "active supervision for the first six months." She referred Linda to the Employment Services Agency for help finding a job, and when staff there terminated their involvement, the officer had Linda return to get additional help finding employment. Another woman's job required working at several apartment sites. The officer forced her to find a new job, where her location could more easily be verified. Sarah, who had more needs than most economic offenders, was also supervised at a high level. Her abusive husband broke her arm at her workplace, and she suffered from depression stemming from a history of child abuse. The officer linked Sarah to a psychiatrist, who provided several months of treatment and referred her to a life skills group. Since Gender Responsive County officers spend more time with the women they supervise, they are more likely to detect and fully address needs.

With economic offenders, Traditional County patterns hold true, starting with limited supervision and quick reductions in or termination of oversight and involvement. Women's violations of conditions are often ignored. I present a few of the many examples where violations were ignored and supervision quickly decreased. Valerie complied with the officer's instructions that she mail in reports in May, June, and September. The officer noted that by September, Valerie had paid no restitution to the grocery store from which she had stolen goods, but the officer took no further action. In another example, Kari's supervising officer noted she owed almost $20,000 in restitution yet earned only $8.25 an hour working as a receptionist. A week later, the officer moved Kari to the most limited supervision status and advised her to inform the judge about her difficulty keeping up with payments. A third woman, Page, had several problems, including irregular employment, an abusive partner, and siblings and friends who used drugs. Yet she received no help through supervision: "There really hasn't been any supervision, not any initiative to help. [I liked] the fact that it ends in about a year, and they took me off mail-in supervision." Traditional County supervising officers had little involvement with economic offenders, even when they violated supervision conditions or had serious problems.

For one-time economic offenders, Gender Responsive County supervision is not always intensive or long lasting. Thus, some one-time economic offenders in both counties complain about unmet needs. In Gender Responsive County, this may happen to women with greater resources and limited troubles. Faith stated that the Gender Responsive County officer provided no help, but described herself as self-sufficient: "[I] already had the skills I needed to get my life back in order after this charge." The criticisms that most characterize Traditional County, especially among women with substantial needs, are "not enough help," "being treated like a number," and "they just want my money." However, as Faith realized, some one-time economic offenders possess adequate resources to solve problems. For them, even Gender Responsive County provides minimal supervision.

Although some one-time economic offenders resent high-level supervision, others appreciate it. One woman welcomed counseling for post-traumatic stress disorder after a friend drowned in an accident unrelated to any illegal activity. Others praised officers for help "setting goals" and "being organized," and for making referrals to job training.

Given their advantaged situations (see chapter 3), I expected positive outcomes for one-time economic offenders. Significantly, the higher-level supervision in Gender Responsive County does not increase incarceration. In fact, it sometimes improves women's lives through mental health, employment, and other services. Similarly, the limited supervision in Traditional County does not necessarily produce failure. It may anger some women to pay fees but receive no help. However, one-time economic offenders generally are able to find work, attend school, leave abusive partners, and live in safe and stable settings. Supervision enhances positive change for them, but it is not as crucial as it is for women in the substance-centered, partner-influenced, and violence-involved subgroups.

MARIJUANA CULTIVATORS

Nine of the twelve women convicted of marijuana cultivation lived in Gender Responsive County. All twelve ended the year in the community without further arrests. Commensurate with fewer problems, supervision was less intense, especially after the first few months. Candace (Gender Responsive County) captured a common theme in this comment to the interviewer: "The PO [was very understanding] of what I need, which was nothing. She was respectful and understanding." Despite the common theme of limited needs and nonintervention, some women mentioned that supervision and other sources did help them. This was a bit more often the case in Gender Responsive County.

Although it never reached the intensity of supervision focused on substance-centered women, supervision of marijuana cultivators increased when officers felt children were in danger or had unmet needs. Officers selectively required parenting classes and reported concerns to child protection workers. Officers responded to slips — e.g., use of marijuana, or failure to complete community service work — with stepped-up requirements for self-help groups, especially Marijuana Anonymous, or other support services.

Due to their fewer problems and greater resources, marijuana cultivators frequently find support and assistance through avenues other than supervision. For instance, one attorney suggested his client attend a drug education program. Also, women often find their own counselors and programs.

A few marijuana cultivators described substantial internal changes due to supervision, other programs or services, or some combination of factors. Supervision helped them find ways to relieve stress other than smoking marijuana. A few other marijuana cultivators felt program referrals and classes were "not helpful," and echoed Candace's sentiment that they did not need assistance. Again, gender-responsive supervision tactics did not seem to have much effect on illegal behavior among these women, but it improved the quality of life of some.

NEEDS-BASED SUPERVISION IN GENDER RESPONSIVE COUNTY

Compared to Traditional County officers, those in Gender Responsive County provide more monitoring and assessment regardless of dominant illegal activity. They identify and address a greater range of needs. Although some women viewed gender-responsive interventions as unnecessary and intrusive, others appreciated the assistance. As I studied women who were least embedded in groups and lifestyles conducive to breaking the law, and who had more human capital and personal resources, I saw an important difference between gender-responsive supervision and the best practices recommended by some correctional experts.

For many experts, the best correctional practice is to concentrate services on meeting needs that predict serious and violent crimes by the highest-risk offenders (Andrews, Bonta, and Hoge 1990). Gender Responsive County supervision concentrates on high-needs women. However, it does not ignore the needs of other women.

In some settings, adequate services for women, both offenders and nonoffenders, in areas such as domestic violence help, substance abuse treatment, and quality employment training could be effective in addressing the needs of women offenders. However, in the absence of a rich service environment, Gender Responsive County officers take up the slack. They do not base eligibility for services on the chance that services will reduce crime. Instead, they provide services on the basis of a holistic assessment of needs. Experts on gender-responsive corrections recommend the holistic approach rather than one focused only on crime reduction.

9

Conclusion:
Key Findings and Implications

Women's social location, social networks, needs, and choices all influence their outcomes at the end of their year of supervision. Additionally, gender-responsive supervision tactics promote positive outcomes. At the same time, traditional supervision may construct misleadingly positive official outcomes. Due to minimal supervision practices, Traditional County officers often do not know when women break laws or violate conditions; the officers also frequently ignore violations. As a result, women may be officially recorded as successes even when they are struggling or failing.

Not all county supervision differences involve gender. The gender-related aspects of supervision are: the emphasis on needs and feelings common to women, supervising officers' relationships with women, empowering women to leave unhealthy relationships with partners, and improvements in women's financial self-sufficiency and independence. Additionally, gender-responsive practices bring women together in groups of women offenders who support each other. The female leaders of these groups and other professionals serve as female role models. Factors unrelated to gender in Gender Responsive County are: high-level supervision of women, emphasis on drug treatment, and graduated sanctions and increasingly intense treatment when women violate conditions of supervision.

GENDER-RELATED DIFFERENCES
BETWEEN THE COUNTIES

Gender Responsive County supervision tactics achieve the gender-responsive ideals of wraparound services and a continuum of care. The county's supervising officers established relationships with women that encouraged and allowed them to divulge their feelings to the officers. The case notes include descriptions of women's feelings and officers' responses. By stressing trust and honesty, the officers promote conversations about problems and how to solve them. In contrast, Traditional County officers rarely create opportunities for interaction. Thus, only Gender Responsive County case notes include examples of women who telephoned officers (sometimes from out of state) or came to the office asking to be taken "off the streets" or for transportation "home." The relationship is a door through which help and change were requested or demanded, and delivered.

Earlier research on drug-involved women shows the positive impact of supervising officers' attention to women's feelings. Women use drugs and alcohol to cope with physical and emotional discomfort and pain from trauma after victimization (Logan et al. 2002; Young, Boyd, and Hubbell 2000). Gender-responsive supervising officers acknowledge and accept women's feelings. They encourage women to discuss their feelings, and even require them to attend programs and groups to explore emotions like grief and anger.

Another unique emphasis in Gender Responsive County is training women for well-paying jobs. This can help end women's dependence on abusive, crime-promoting men. A major impetus for preparing women for work is the employment counselor who works at the community supervision offices. Gender Responsive County officers also offer advice to steer women toward self-sufficiency. Several examples from case notes follow.

> [Nan] said she was not working because she was helping to finance her partner's business. I told her she needs to find her own employment.
> I talked about constant crises in [Shannon's] life. I told her she and her husband need to take some positive action — need to go to appointments and groups. If they kept appointments and attended groups, they would learn to deal with problems better.
> [Jo] states things are not going well with her boyfriend. He is running around with someone else. Told her to concentrate on her situation and finding an acceptable place to live.
> I told [Meredith] that rather than sleeping on the couch in her sister's cramped house, I would rather see her get an apartment on her own.

Such examples can be found only in the Gender Responsive County notes. Women's movement toward self-sufficiency lessens their vulnerability to abuse and oppression based on dependent relationships with people who hurt them, and pressure them to engage in crime and drug use.

DIFFERENCES BETWEEN THE COUNTIES
UNRELATED TO GENDER

This book presents considerable evidence that Gender Responsive County is unique in promoting a chain of interventions from detection of drug use through substance-abuse aftercare treatment. The sequence includes drug testing, in-person contact, sudden strikes by officers in response to drug use, a wide variety of graduated sanctions and treatments, formal substance abuse evaluations and reevaluations, and financial assistance for evaluation and treatment.

Research on other populations confirms that drug use promotes crime, and suggests the benefits of a high investment in efforts to stop drug use. One study concluded that "cocaine and heroin use creates an earnings imperative that directly impels remunerative crime" (Uggen and Thompson 2003, 151). Drug use pushes women into prostitution, which leads them to use even more drugs to increase their "confidence, control, and closeness to others and to decrease feelings of guilt and sexual distress" (Young, Boyd, and Hubbell 2000, 789). Research showing that drugs bring people into contact with criminal networks provides further support for the connection of drug use to other crime (Schroeder, Giordano, and Cernkovich 2007).

THE APPLICABILITY OF FINDINGS TO
OTHER SUPERVISION AGENCIES

The present research compares community supervision in two particular counties. However, my prior research on Gender Responsive County showed that it typified best practices for gender-responsive corrections (Morash, Bynum, and Koons 1996). Additionally, other researchers have examined sites with supervision similar to that delivered in Traditional County. Chan et al. summarize results of multiple studies:

> Traditional postrelease supervision regarding substance abuse has largely consisted of limited attention to and monitoring of offender recidivism and drug use. Infrequent drug testing, brief infrequent phone or in-person contact, and lack of coordination and provision of substance abuse treatment have characterized the norm in supervision strategies for persons with substance abuse disorders. (2005, 448–49)

Research documents this pattern of sporadic, limited supervision in several areas of the United States (Center on Addiction and Substance Abuse 1998; Kleinman et al. 2003; Prendergast, Wellisch, and Falkin 1995). A study in England likewise finds that probation officers leave women and men largely to their own devices as they face various obstacles (Farrall 2003, 250–52). Limited and narrow supervision occurs widely both inside and outside of the United States.

Other researchers find deficiencies in traditional approaches to community supervision for women offenders (Festervan 2003; Little Hoover Commission 2004; McMahon 2000). A study in Cook County, Illinois, shows that probation officers believe there is a need for "training about gender-specific needs and other topics related to female probationers," and the officers recommend additional training in "communication and interviewing skills, resource development and special techniques for working with women probationers, especially female drug users" (Seng and Lurigio 2005, 81). Consistent with the approach in Gender Responsive County, Cook County officers favored a specialized women's unit to "give officers more time to broker resources and focus on women's issues."

Criminal justice researchers conceptualize community supervision as oriented toward law enforcement or social casework, or as a mixture of these approaches (Paparozzi and Gendreau 2005). Neither Gender Responsive County nor Traditional County uses a strictly law enforcement or social casework approach. Gender Responsive County applies both approaches heavily. Traditional County uses a combination of sporadic law enforcement with sporadic social casework; many women were little touched or affected by either one. This study provides evidence to confirm the effectiveness of the Gender Responsive County mix of monitoring, graduated sanctions, needs assessment, and multiple treatment interventions (Andrews and Kiessling 1980; Paparozzi and Gendreau 2005). The evidence supports my finding that the mix promotes positive outcomes.

THE CONSTRUCTION OF OUTCOMES

In this book's introduction, I raised the concern that elements of intensive community supervision in Gender Responsive County could contribute to increased incarceration. In other words, supervision practices could turn relatively positive cases into official failures. I did find that greater numbers of substance-centered women in Gender Responsive County were in and out of jail for brief sanctions. However, increased treatment, not lengthy incarceration, typically followed. In Traditional County, once women reached a tipping point in drug use and noncompliance with supervision requirements, revocation and incarceration followed. Gender-responsive supervision did not result in women's spending more time in jail and prison. Traditional County tended to revoke women's community supervision and to use incarceration instead of treatment. Gender Responsive County used more treatment than punishment.

I described a subset of Traditional County women with the phrase *little known and little happening*, due to limited and narrow supervision. For this group, supervision tactics may construct an official record of success for women who actually engage in undetected crime. Earlier research ignores connections between limited and narrow supervision and misleading official constructions of success. A full understanding of the effects of supervision requires studying outcomes such as engagement with treatment and independence from negative influences, as well as the official records of success.

Sanctions of jail and incarceration are imprecise indicators of failure. Especially when coupled with treatment opportunities and abstinence, they may in fact become positive turning points. In a few cases, women saw incarceration as life saving: "tough" supervising officers got them "off the streets" and away from dangerous drugs.

EXCESSIVE CONTROL OF WOMEN

Chapter 1 raised the possibility that gender-responsive programming increases controls over women, with no benefit. On the contrary, my research found that many women appreciated the greater monitoring in Gender Responsive County. Greater controls contributed to the women's leaving very destructive situations and making positive changes.

I question whether one aspect of intervention and control is just and beneficial, however. The data for both counties contain a few examples of supervising officers' blurring the responsibilities of child protective services, officially delivered by the Child and Family Services Agency, with control and punishment administered through the community supervision offices. The following examples suggest that supervising officers punished women primarily to protect children.

One officer reported to a Child and Family Services Agency worker that a woman with an infant in her care regularly used methamphetamines. The officer also revoked the woman's supervision, so the woman spent most of the year in jail. (Gender Responsive County)

After discovering that a pregnant woman had used methamphetamines, the officer noted "next use, I will put her in jail until the baby is born." (Traditional County)

By law, supervising officers must report suspected child endangerment and abuse to child protective services agencies. However, they go beyond the law when they punish women for endangering children. Since the research did not uniformly collect data on this topic, I do not know how often officers exerted control over women to protect children or fetuses. The women described above and a few others expressed anger at being "locked up" and "not helped" when officers acted primarily to protect their children. Feminist theorists criticize the justice system for exerting unwarranted control over women to regulate reproduction—i.e., protect fetuses—and enforce standards of motherhood (Boyd 1999, 2000; Smart and Smart 1978). Whether and how often this occurs under various approaches to supervision is an important area for future research and debate. Ultimately, the justice of controlling women to protect children depends on the authorized powers of supervising officers.

DESISTING FROM DRUG USE AND CRIME

Understanding desistence from crime requires knowing how women transition to legal behavior and lifestyles (Uggen and Kruttschnitt 1998, 339). Key transition points include improvements in social networks, education, training, work, and lifestyle. Although access to resources is important, it is insufficient without internal changes that include cognitive transformations in "identity and changes in the meaning and desirability of deviant/criminal behavior itself" (Giordano, Cernkovich, and Rudolph 2002, 992; also see Farrall and Bowling 1999; Kearney 1998; Laub and Sampson 2001; Maruna 2000; O'Brien 2001; O'Brien and Harm 2002; Piliavin, Gartner, and Thornton 1986; Sampson and Laub 1993; Shover 1996; Shover and Thompson 1992).

The crucial areas of positive change depend on women's dominant illegal activity. One-time economic offenders desist simply by resuming noncriminal behavior patterns. For women with limited criminality—those convicted of growing marijuana or child maltreatment—desistance involves stopping these acts. For substance-centered women, violent women, and those influenced by their partners, desistance requires much more complex changes in lifestyle, social location, and self.

Learning to cope with negative feelings and developing problem solving skills stand out in the present study as particularly important internal changes for the most disadvantaged women. Research on addictions confirms the importance of change in these areas (Kearney 1998; McKay et al. 2006; Walitzer and Dearing 2006). In the counties I studied, women described learning that anger is not "all bad" and how to deal with it effectively; recognizing feelings and controlling reactions; and learning "how to deal with things when you're real upset." Flo, from Traditional County, said she had suffered from depression since the age of sixteen. She learned to control her anxiety, improved her communication skills, and learned how to describe her feelings without "just breaking down and crying." One woman explicitly linked stopping drug use to learning how to cope by "talking"; she said her supervision "helped me learn to handle things by talking about it instead of using drugs." Coping also requires problem solving skills like breaking problems down into "rational steps"—in the words of Jen, from Gender Responsive County—and gaining "tools to deal with people [and knowing] what to watch for," as Holly, of Gender Responsive County, put it. Meetings with supervising officers, groups, and treatment programs increase women's capacity to cope. Better coping skills help women take advantage of social networks and training and employment opportunities.

A study of Chicago women paroled from prison provides further evidence of the dual influence of resources and internal changes (O'Brien 2001; also see O'Brien and Harm 2002). Internal changes in self-efficacy, coping skills, and resilience contributed to positive outcomes. Key external resources were safe and affordable housing, positive relationships, rewarding employment, sufficient earnings, and positive community ties. These findings reinforce the conclusions of the present research.

Also consistent with my findings about how women change is Kearney's (1998) reanalysis of qualitative data from ten studies of women in drug recovery. The neediest women she studied were most like my substance-centered group. Formal treatment programs were essential to their recovery. Change started when the women realized that drugs caused more distress than they relieved. It continued when distress became acute, and treatment was readily available. The capacity to keep a job, stay out of jail, stay healthy, and have child custody further motivated abstinence. Keeping busy, in some cases by filling time with treatment and self-help meetings, provided social support and physical places where women could avoid pressures to use drugs. Women who recovered eventually learned to care and advocate for themselves.

In Gender Responsive County, high levels of monitoring and frequent detection, followed by progressively punitive sanctions, attached unpleasant consequences to the use of drugs and alcohol. These supervision tactics heighten women's awareness of the downside of use, which Kearney found promoted positive change. Gender Responsive County tactics also channel women toward interesting and well-paying jobs, require them to "fill time" with numerous meetings, and in other ways promote the changes that Kearney found lead to abstinence. Finally, Kearny and I both found the same typical sequence of getting treatment, then abstaining from drugs, followed by other positive changes.

Kearney (1998, 509) described the women who had the greatest difficulty recovering from drug addiction and dependence. Like the substance-centered women I studied, these women had experienced deprivation and abuse during childhood and had difficulty identifying and coping with emotions, parenting burdens, intimate partner violence, and limited education. Kearney found that the more compatible available treatment was with a woman's cultural perspective, the greater the likelihood she would persist in treatment. Only the Native American women in the counties I studied specifically commented on this as an aspect of positive treatment experiences. However, other women compared helpful and nonhelpful treatment programs and supervision experiences. Their comments also support Kearney's finding that appropriate person-to-program matches promote positive outcomes.

Taken together, the analysis presented in this book and evidence from earlier studies support the gender-responsive ideal of wraparound services and a continuum of care (Festervan 2003; Gutiérrez and Lewis 1999; Zaplin 1998). O'Brien and Harm recommend a social work approach called empowerment practice, to simultaneously help people in need and attack "social ills that relate to individual behaviors" (2002, 311). Supervising officers and other professionals can advocate for women and at the same time open up opportunities for jobs, education, and treatment. Gender Responsive County officers, for example, even provide concrete financial help for program fees and basic needs to counteract extreme disadvantage. This person-by-person approach is helpful in overcoming disadvantages linked to broader social structure. Yet it is not a replacement for public policies to prevent and ameliorate the effects of childhood abuse, domestic violence, and poverty. Ironically, as I discuss below in a section on policy and program recommendations, some public policies make things worse for women, and contribute to the social ills that supervising officers must help women overcome.

WOMEN'S AGENCY

Even given the information on internal change and external resources provided by this study, I cannot always explain why some women but not others stopped breaking the law. Maher's research on women involved in drugs, prostitution, and other crimes challenges "myths about women's passivity and submissiveness — whether 'natural' or socially induced" (2000, 2). The women she studied "perceive themselves neither as powerless victims nor as emancipated and independent, nor, as their own accounts demonstrate, are they without agency" (19). Cognizant of this perspective, I searched the data for the ways that the women in my study drove their own year-end outcomes. By absconding, moving, and insulating themselves from supervision and treatment, some women immunized themselves against the efforts of supervising officers and others. Alternatively, when supervision was limited, some women found effective alternative interventions. Even though they exercised personal agency, substance-centered and partner-influenced women were especially constrained by their social standing, disadvantages, and problems.

INEQUALITY AND JUSTICE

Consistent with national trends, African American and Native American women were overrepresented on probation and parole caseloads in both counties. This is the case even though drug use often accounts for women's involvement with the justice system, and African American and white rates of drug use are about the same (Substance Abuse and Mental Health Services Administration 2002). (People of Native American and Puerto Rican origin have higher rates of illicit drug use than do whites.) Poverty partially explains the discrepancy: middle-class and affluent users of illegal drugs can afford to get treatment or counseling on their own, or simply grow out of drug use, while poor people more often become entangled with the justice system (Biernacki 1986; Granfield and Cloud 1999; Wu and Ringwalt 2005). Advantaged women are able to stay out of court by using relatives' and their own resources, including money and information, to facilitate access to treatment. Police drug enforcement concentrates on poor communities, where drug activity is more likely to occur in public places (Boyd 1999, 50). This brings more poor women into court.

Taking a public health perspective, Moore and Elkavich (2008) decry the negative effects on individuals and communities of incarceration for drug-related offenses. They recommend alternatives, such as drug courts (National Institute of Justice 2006), judicial exercise of discretion in the use of community alternatives, and release of drug offenders on parole. Mental health courts also keep people out of jails and prisons (Huddleston, Marlowe, and Casebolt 2008).

Although shifting toward more community-based corrections may decrease the overrepresentation of poor racial and ethnic minorities in prisons and jails, it cannot level the playing field. Without other changes, there will still be barriers to treatment access. Research confirms that, nationwide, child-care responsibilities and the inability to pay limit treatment options for lower income people (Brady and Ashley 2005, 1). I found that especially in Gender Responsive County, officers had to spend considerable time encouraging women or advocating for them to get insurance, evaluations, and program services. Economic offenders who were slightly better off could use psychiatric and other mental health services to limit their involvement with the justice system. As a result, professionals labeled economic offenders' crimes as related to mental health, and therefore appropriately dealt with through private mental health care. In contrast, I identified some substance-centered women who had such severe mental illness that their supervising officers and others felt the correctional system lacked the ability to house them or meet their needs. Reliant on public services, these women may go without needed evaluation or treatment. Getting more women out of prisons and jails and onto community supervision caseloads does not ensure equal access to substance abuse treatment, mental health treatment, housing, and so on.

For substance-centered women, who constitute more than half of the probation and parole caseloads, what is the appropriate role for the criminal justice system? Decriminalization of addiction is not on the horizon in the United States, so substance-centered women will continue to flood into the courts. It is imperative, therefore, to determine how to respond to substance-centered women within the correctional system to make their lives better, not worse. The research described in this book confirms that implementing gender-responsive programming ideals in community corrections is a step in the right direction.

IMPLICATIONS FOR THEORY AND RESEARCH

Since current U.S. policy addresses the drug problems of the poor largely through the criminal justice system, research on substance-centered women must be integrated with research on addiction and recovery. Recognizing the strong connection of trauma to women's drug use (Ladwig and Andersen 1989; Vogt 1998), early models of addiction treatment specific to women emphasized alternatives for dealing with trauma. The models suggested that female staff experienced in overcoming trauma-induced addiction act as role models. Recent research has shown that effective treatment programs for substance abuse address problems common to women, provide female therapists, focus exclusively on women, and encourage long treatment periods (Brady and Ashley 2005; Claus et al. 2007; Covington 1999; Greenfield et al. 2007; Veysey et al. 2007). Future research on women who break the law largely because of drugs or alcohol must consider theories of addiction and recovery in explaining offenders' actions and ultimate outcomes.

Particularly for substance-centered women, a one-year outcome study is inadequate. My analysis identified a small number of women who had just started turning their lives around near the end of the year, and a larger group still using drugs, but avoiding other illegal acts and making positive changes. The precarious situations of some women who abstained from drugs all year suggest the likelihood of failure after the study ends. Long-term follow-up, though, is expensive and difficult due to the women's high degree of mobility. An alternative method is retrospective interviews to compare women with similar crimes and backgrounds who are succeeding or failing three to five years after supervision began (Fetterman 1998; Ruspini 2002).

Some illegal activity subgroups deserve more research attention than I can provide, due to my small sample size. Verifying and expanding my findings about partner-influenced women could be very useful. Richie (1996) conducted a fuller study of African American women entrapped in relationships with men. Her findings suggest partner-influenced women are more common in some racial and ethnic groups, or in jail populations. Gender-responsive tactics that empower entangled or partner-influenced women to leave criminal and abusive men could profitably be studied to show specifically how such programming helps women break away. Repeat economic offenders also deserve more study. Daly (1992) identified two motivations — greed and coping with poverty — for women's economic crimes. I found women influenced by each of these motivations. Proclivities toward greed are probably best addressed through efforts to convince potential economic offenders of the costs, harm, and consequences of crime. Programming like "theft talks," "penitentiary tours," and punishments could be evaluated for effectiveness. Research also can clarify the effects of poverty on economic offenders; the aim would be to identify policies, such as public benefits and insurance, that could be changed to reduce poverty as a risk.

The study's findings inform theoretical understanding of desisting from crime. For men, multiple studies show that marriage promotes desistance (Horney et al. 1995; Laub, Nagin, and Sampson 1998; Warr 1998; also see the thorough review by Huebner 2007). Giordano, Cernkovich, and Schroeder (2007) conclude that some spouses provided previously law-breaking women with good role models for handling their feelings and avoiding violence and other illegal acts. I question suppositions that marriage has a consistently positive influence. A literature review on desistance from drug and alcohol use concludes that women are more likely to relapse on alcohol if they are married (Walitzer and Dearing 2006). This is probably due to that fact that partners' alcohol consumption creates stress and marital conflict. The review further concludes that marriage is likely to have negative effect on women taking illegal drugs. Griffin and Armstrong

(2003) similarly find that living with a man does not promote women's desistance from crime. In fact, women living with husbands or boyfriends are more likely than other women to deal drugs. In my research, intimate partners ranged from abusive, criminal men to those who substantially improved women's quality of life by contributing income and other positive support. Connection to a partner is a useless variable on its own in research on women's desistance. It should be replaced by evidence of partners' behavior and level of support for avoiding crime.

For substance-centered women, the order of events is not becoming involved with noncriminal and supportive men, and then ending illegal behavior. Women first get clean, and then they make other improvements, possibly including connections with nonabusive, sober, law-abiding partners. Acquiring such a partner, though, is not necessary for success. Women can find alternative sources of support in relationships with relatives, supervising officers, professionals, treatment and self-help groups, and other women. Future assessments of correctional programs for women should consider the sequence of change, the connection of resources to internal changes, and the combination of resources and internal changes necessary for positive outcomes.

Many studies and much theorizing about desistance from drug use and crime omit the criminal justice system itself as an influence. I placed the system, specifically probation and parole, at the center. Supervising officers' tactics play an important part in constructing and producing outcomes. Depending on the tactics used, supervision varies in its impact on drug use and crime.

IMPLICATIONS FOR LOCAL
CORRECTIONAL PRACTICE

My findings and the results of other research support the central role of relationships to women's success under supervision. They also suggest that for substance-centered women, effective supervising officers carry out many of the functions of a case manager in substance abuse treatment.

Women's lasting, positive relationships with other program participants, program and agency staff, and supervising officers contribute substantially to their success. Gilligan's (1982) seminal work showing the centrality of relationships to girls' and women's development and well-being lends validity to this finding. My study findings are also consistent with Covington's (1998; Covington and Surrey 1997) conclusion that relationships are central in women offenders' recovery from trauma and addiction.

Several Gender Responsive County tactics are used in intensive case management, a service delivery method in addictions treatment (Arfken et al. 2003). In particular, Gender Responsive County supervising officers, like case managers, require drug and alcohol assessments, implement recommended plans, connect women to services, and then monitor the adequacy of services (Austin and McLelland 1994). Not all studies support case managers' effectiveness for all offenders (Chan et al. 2005), but some provide evidence of its effectiveness for women offenders (Jessup et al. 2001; Siefert and Pimlott 2001). Frequent contact and long-term treatment increase case managers' effectiveness (Longshore, Turner, and Fain 2005). These elements of successful case management are integrated into Gender Responsive County's supervision.

The smaller, more affluent population and lower crime rate in Gender Responsive County has relevance to replicating the county's model for supervision. Although the differences were not extreme, the county's advantages may have facilitated putting into practice the ideals of gender-responsive corrections. The availability of funding for evaluations, treatment, and housing was crucial to some women's success. Replication elsewhere would depend on adequate resources.

Reproducing the good results of the gender-responsive approach also depends on staff training and skills. To develop strong relationships and promote drug treatment, gender-responsive supervising officers needed special skills. They knew how to network with community resources; relate to women; and appropriately mix monitoring, sanctioning, encouraging, and providing treatment. These abilities enabled the gender-responsive officers to implement wraparound services adapted to women's individual needs. Additionally, the officers' determination, character, and understanding of women's lives would need to be reproduced in other settings.

Tribal resources increased program access for Native American women. Other communities might use this resource model to provide comprehensive services to their members. As an added benefit, tribal services helped women develop a positive ethnic identity and integrate into an ethnic network. A service model oriented to an ethnic group may not be relevant to all women, particularly those unattached to a specific group or community. However, the Native American network of services is a positive example worth considering for other communities.

NEEDED REFORMS IN PROGRAMS AND POLICIES

As a society, we need to invest more in protecting children from adversity. Childhood abuse and exposure to violence in families and communities contribute to violence, drug use, crime, depression, and suicide in adults (Centers for Disease Control and Prevention 2005; Felitti et al. 1998). The lives of the women I studied provide evidence of failure to prevent childhood adversity for them and, in many cases, for their children. Economists argue that in the long run, it costs less to prevent childhood adversity than to address the resulting negative outcomes through treatment (Kilburn and Karoly 2008). Prevention also minimizes human suffering and destruction. Mothers on probation and parole sorely need services to address their own negative childhoods and to protect their children from similar adversity.

For the women in my study, it appeared that welfare reforms of past decades had the intended effect of reducing public benefit populations. The 1996 Welfare Reform Act, Temporary Assistance for Needy Families (TANF), imposed a lifetime ban on cash assistance and food stamps for people convicted of state or federal felony offenses involving the use or sale of drugs. A study of San Francisco mothers who used drugs showed this policy had decreased financial assistance and quality of life for them, and increased their use of crime to obtain money (Murphy and Sales 2001). Employment and legal earnings had not increased, as had been hoped. Given their extreme economic disadvantages, the absence of substance-centered women from public benefit rolls in my research is striking. TANF should be redesigned so that it does not stand as a barrier to women's recovery from substance addiction.

The federal Adoption and Safe Families Act of 1997 requires termination of parental rights once children have been in foster care for fifteen months. The aim is to speed up child custody decisions. For the women I studied, the result was often to permanently end custody and contact, thereby removing reuniting with children as a motive for mothers' positive change. Federal public housing policy permits, and in some cases requires, housing programs to deny access to people convicted or suspected of drug use. Since the 1990s, prisoners cannot obtain Pell Grants to cover education costs, and people convicted of drug offenses are ineligible for other federally supported education programs. At the state level, even the relatively effective state insurance program (described in chapter 1) left women with inadequate or delayed insurance coverage for substance abuse or mental health evaluations and treatment. These policies all increase the odds against women offenders.

Public policies that deny benefits to offenders remind them that they are stigmatized, unsalvageable, throw-away women. Theorists (Bourdieu 1977; Link and Phelan 2001) recognize that people without resources are most often stigmatized, and that the stigmatization further limits their resources. In my study, the generally more advantaged economic, child-maltreatment, and marijuana-cultivating offenders consistently felt least stigmatized. In fact, they actively rejected stigma, insisting that they had done nothing to warrant arrest and that they were not the "kind of people" who should be supervised. Highly disadvantaged and marginalized substance-centered women felt most stigmatized. Programs and policies reinforced the stigmatization.

Effective policies and programs integrate women into nonstigmatizing services. Agnes's experience in Gender Responsive County provides a good example. The supervising officer required Agnes, then nineteen years old, to meet with an employment counselor, who advised her to enroll in the Program for Young Parents. This program focuses on counseling, GED preparation, child care, and financial assistance. Agnes told the interviewer that the program gave her "emotional support and financial support, and [they] have faith in you." The counselor helped her through her drug use and was very supportive. Once Agnes stopped using drugs, she earned her GED and made plans to enter another program that would give her income and provide further training. By relying on this program as the primary intervention, the supervising officer addressed Agnes's needs. She increased her opportunity for financial independence and matched the programming to Agnes's stage in life. The program was a good match because it steered Agnes from strictly correctional programming to a broad set of community resources. In this case, federally supported programming, in combination with gender-responsive supervision practices, contributed to a young woman's capacity to turn her life around. Other nonstigmatizing policies include guaranteed family income, universal health care that covers substance abuse and mental health treatment, and alternatives to permanently severing mother-child relationships (Murphy and Sales 2001).

We are at a critical juncture for implementing effective community corrections programs for women. With federal support, many states are further reducing prison populations by increasing the numbers of offenders on probation and parole. Governors and legislators realize that the financial and social costs of incarceration are too high in relation to the benefits. As a result, the need for community programs and services is growing, while an economic recession contributes to cuts in social and mental health services. Many individuals under court supervision lack medical insurance to cover physical, mental, and substance abuse evaluation and treatment. It is unknown whether the hoped-for reform in the U.S. health care system will meet their needs. Though it would be most cost-effective and just to abandon policies that ban women from housing, education grants, and public support, there seems to be a lack of political will and courage to take these steps. Legislators fear upsetting conservative forces that promote punishment over the women's lifetime. Given this context, carefully designed and implemented gender-responsive program models provide a local solution to the larger problem of inadequate services and accumulated harmful, punitive policies. Programs like Gender Responsive County's community corrections enable women to improve their lives and to escape the forces that promote drug use and crime.

APPENDIXES

Survey Questions for Supervising Officers

OFFICER SURVEY AT THE BEGINNING OF SUPERVISION

Does the probationer or parolee have a juvenile record? If yes, did she ever spend time in a juvenile institution or facility? What was the longest period of time spent in a juvenile institution?

How long have you been the primary person with the probationer or parolee for this referral?

For the following, would you rate this woman as much higher, higher, slightly higher, about the same, slightly lower, lower, or much lower on the following: Compared to other women under supervision, how likely is she to become reinvolved in breaking the law? Compared to other women under supervision, what level of supervision and oversight is this woman receiving from your staff or places you refer her to?

Does the probationer or parolee express hostility toward the criminal justice system-in other words, does she say that her violations of the law are okay?

Is the client's attitude toward convention unfavorable?

Does the probationer or parolee believe her sentence is invalid?

Compared to other women in the program, to what extent does she have personal problems that are related to her breaking the law-for example, history of abuse, involvement in negative relationships, addiction to drugs, learning problems, and limited education (much greater extent, greater extent, slightly greater extent, about the same extent, slightly less extent, less extent, much less extent)?

OFFICER SURVEY AFTER ONE YEAR OF SUPERVISION

Has she been arrested in the last year? How many times? Explain the most serious result.

Has she been convicted of any crimes in the last year? How many times? Explain the most serious result.

Has she been charged with any violations of conditions of supervision? How many times? Explain the most serious result.

Has she had any revocations [termination of probation or parole status followed by incarceration in jail or prison]? What was the most serious result?

Did she do any of these, or other things: failure to meet payment schedule, failure to report truthfully or notify the supervising officer as directed, failure to follow directives of court or supervising officer, prohibited use of alcohol or drugs, possession of controlled substance, irregular or unsuccessful participation in treatment programs, absconded supervision, refusal to comply with imposed sanctions, new nonperson misdemeanor offense, new DUII [driving under the influence of intoxicants] offense, new nonperson felony offense, prohibited contact with minors/victims/survivors, possession or use of a dangerous or deadly weapon, new person to person offense?

Has she appeared in court for any other reasons not already noted? How many times? For what?

For the following, did community supervision staff get information about the listed areas? For each, did the community supervision staff try to help her with this need? Did the community supervision staff directly provide help and/or make a referral? Educational needs, such as to get a degree or learn basic math and reading skills; special learning problems, like a learning disability; need for drug or alcohol education or treatment; mental health; sexual abuse as a child; other physical abuse as a child; abuse by an intimate partner; general health needs for treatment or education; HIV/AIDS education or treatment; pregnancy care or education; job skills/education; child custody or care needs; housing needs; life skills-for example, money management; parenting skills.

Interview Questions for Women on Probation or Parole

INITIAL INTERVIEW

Income

In the past thirty days, how much money did you receive from all legal sources, such as wages, food stamps, or welfare? Does this amount include income from your husband, boyfriend, or other family members? How much is your total income, and how much is from other people?

In the past thirty days, how much money did you receive from all illegal sources?

Children

Based on a list of your children, what ages are they, where have they been living in the last six months, and if not with you, how much contact have you had in the last six months? If they moved, why?

Work

In the last six months, have you worked at a paying job? If yes, was the job in prison? How many different jobs, and were they in prison? What kind of work did you do for your highest paying job? How much did you make a week, and how many weeks were you working? How many hours a week did you work? Are you working now? If not, can you explain? If yes, what kind of job do or did you do? For all jobs in the past six months, how many hours a week did you work, how many weeks did you work, and how much were you paid each week?

School

Based on a list of school programs, programs to learn a trade, programs to get a degree, or programs to improve basic reading and math skills in the last six months, what was the program name? What was it for? How many weeks did it last? How many hours a week did you attend? Are you currently attending? If not currently attending, why not?

Relationship with Partner

For any part of the last six months, have you been involved in a regular dating, live-in situation, or marriage with a man or woman? If yes, a man or a woman? For how much of the six months? Was this with the same person? In the last six months, have you had a date, husband, or partner physically hurt you on purpose in any way-for example, hit or punch, slap, bite, choke, or sexually attack you? If yes, what was the most serious injury that resulted? How often did this person hurt you? The choices are: daily, weekly, monthly, less than monthly but more than once in six months, once in six months.

In the last six months, did a date, husband, or partner get you in trouble with the law or probation/parole violations? If yes, how many times? What was the most serious result? For that time, how did the person get you in trouble?

Mental Health

Have you ever been evaluated by a psychologist or psychiatrist, or anyone else, for a mental health problem? If yes, was this in jail or prison?

Have you ever spent time in a mental health hospital or overnight mental health program? If yes, was this while incarcerated? How many times? What was the longest you stayed in a mental health hospital or overnight program? Did you voluntarily agree to stay?

Are you currently under the care of a psychologist or psychiatrist, or some other person who helped you with mental illness? If yes, for how long?

Were you ever given legal drugs to help you with mental health problems? Did you voluntarily agree to take these? Were you incarcerated at the time?

Juvenile and Criminal History

Do you have a juvenile record?

Were you ever placed outside your home for each of these reasons: truancy, runaway, incorrigibility, or something else? If something else, what was it?

Did you ever spend time in each of the following: a detention center, training school, group home, or foster home? What was the longest period of time you spent in a juvenile institution?

How old were you when you were arrested for the first time? By arrest, I mean any time you were booked or fingerprinted. What were you arrested for?

Substance Abuse

Answer these questions for each of the drugs: alcohol, tobacco, marijuana, powder cocaine, crack cocaine, heroin, PCP/angel dust, amphetamines, downers, Quaaludes, street methadone, crystal meth, valium or tranquilizers, LSD/acid, ecstasy, inhalants. Have you ever tried the drug?

When you first tried it, how old were you? Have you used it in the last six months? How many days in the past thirty days? In the last six months, have you consciously tried to cut down or quit using it on your own? Have you felt that you needed or were dependent on it in the past six months? Are you now receiving treatment or detox for it? Have you received treatment or detox for it in the past? Do you feel you could use treatment for it?

Were you tested for drug use during the last six months? If yes, how often? Were you routinely tested or tested because your probation or parole officer thought you were high or using?

Did you have any urine tests come back positive for drugs? How many times?

Social Networks
When you are upset or worried about something, who do you talk to? Who do you feel really cares about you? (People named are coded as providing emotional support.)

Who do you spend your time with, hang out with? (People named are coded as providing social support.)

Who would you ask if you needed something, like help doing something or money, or help with caring for family members? If you need help with school work, or help at your job, who would you ask? (People named are coded as providing instrumental help.)

For each person named, what is the person's sex? What is the person's relationship to you? How old is the person? How frequently do you have contact? The choices are: yearly, a few times a year, monthly, weekly, daily. Is this person not important, somewhat important, or very important to you? What is the most serious offense committed by this person? Was the person ever arrested?

YEAR-END INTERVIEW ON SITUATION AND CIRCUMSTANCES SINCE THE INITIAL INTERVIEW

Place of Residence
Where did you live since the last interview? Who did you live with?

About how many weeks did you live at a residential program or in transitional housing?

If you moved, can you explain your living situation? What was the reason for the changes in your living arrangements? How long did you live at each location?

Income, Children, Work, School, Relationship with Partner, Mental Health, Social Networks

The questions from the initial interview were repeated for the past year.

Illegal Activity

Have you been arrested or convicted? Have you committed other new crimes? If yes, how many times? For what? What was the most serious result for each type of offense?

Have you been charged with violating any conditions of your probation or parole? Have you had any revocations as a result?

Have you appeared in court for any other reasons that we have not talked about?

Substance Abuse

The questions from the initial interview were repeated for the past year.

If you tested positive for drugs, what happened to you each time that you tested positive for drugs? Were you terminated from a program, but then allowed to return? Which program(s)?

Were you terminated from a program permanently? Which program(s)? Did you have more restrictions-for example, more testing, more frequent reporting, tether, requirements to live in a residential setting? Did you have to work with more or different staff? Did you have to go to another program, or an additional program? Did you get jail time? How many days? Did something else happen? What?

Experiences in Programs

Which of the programs over the last year-including seeing your probation or parole officer as part of your supervision, or a program that you participated in while on supervision, or a program that the PO [probation or parole officer] referred you to-do you feel has involved or helped you the most?

What is the name of the program? How did you find out about it?

For each area listed below, did staff at the most helpful program get this information from you? Did staff at that program try to help you with this? Did staff at that program refer you to another program or person to help you with this? Educational needs, such as to get a degree or learn basic math and reading skills; special learning problems, like a learning disability; need for drug or alcohol education or treatment; mental health; sexual abuse as a child;

other physical abuse as a child; abuse by an intimate partner; general health needs for treatment or education; HIV/AIDS education or treatment; pregnancy care or education; job skills/education; child custody or care needs; housing needs; life skills-for example, money management; parenting skills.

For the program that was most helpful to you, did any of these things happen? How often? Did you drop out of the program? Did you receive any poor evaluations while in the program?

Did you have any violations of probation or parole? Did you miss appointments or required activities? Did you receive an award or certificate? Did you participate in any type of graduation ceremony? Did the number of times you needed to report to staff decrease because staff thought you were doing well on your own? Did the number of times you were drug tested decrease?

Did you break any rules in programs you were in? If yes, what happened: Were you terminated from a program, but then allowed to return? Were you terminated from a program permanently? Did you have more restrictions-for example, more testing, more frequent reporting, tether, requirements to live in a residential setting? Did you have to work with more or different staff? Did you have to go to another program, or an additional program? Did you get jail time? How many days? Did something else happen? What?

Do you feel that the program that you found most helpful helped you overall? Why or why not?

What did you like most about it? What did you like least? What are the most important skills you learned? What changes do you think would have made it better? In what ways is it different than other ones you have been sent to or attended?

Allard, P. 2002. *Life sentences: Denying welfare benefits to women convicted of drug offenses*. Washington: Sentencing Project.

Andrews, D. A., J. Bonta, and R. D. Hoge. 1990. Classification for effective rehabilitation: Rediscovering psychology. *Criminal Justice and Behavior* 17:19–52.

Andrews, D. A., and J. J. Kiessling. 1980. Program structure and effective correctional practice: A summary of CaVic research. In *Effective correctional treatment*, edited by R. Ross and P. Gendreau, 439–63. Toronto: Butterworths.

Anglin, M. D., and G. Speckart. 1988. Narcotics use and crime: A multisample, multimethod analysis. *Criminology* 26:197–233.

Arfken, C. L., C. Klein, E. J. Agius, and S. di Menza. 2003. Implementation of selected target cities components: Analysis of matching, case management, and linkages. In *Clinical assessment and substance abuse treatment: The target cities experience*, edited by R. C. Stephens, C. K. Scott, and R. D. Muck, 103–28. Albany: State University of New York Press.

Austin, C. D., and R. W. McLelland. 1994. Case management in human services: Reflections on public policy. *Journal of Case Management* 6:119–26.

Austin, J., B. Bloom, and T. Donahue. 1992. *Female offenders in the community: An analysis of innovative strategies and programs*. Washington: National Institute of Corrections.

Bates, R. 2001. *Improving outcomes for children and families of incarcerated parents*. Chicago: University of Illinois at Chicago, Jane Addams College of Social Work.

Belknap, J. 1996. *The invisible woman*. Belmont, Mass.: Wadsworth.

Bertrand, M. A. 1999. Incarceration as a gendering strategy. *Canadian Journal of Law and Society* 14:47–59.

Biernacki, P. 1986. *Pathways from heroin addiction: Recovery without treatment*. Philadelphia: Temple University Press.

Bloom, B., B. Owen, and S. S. Covington. 2004. Women offenders and the gendered effects of public policy. *Review of Policy Research* 21:31–48.

——— and M. S. Raeder. 2003. *Gender-responsive strategies: Research, practice, and guiding principles for women offenders*. Washington: National Institute of Corrections.

Bloom, B., and D. Steinhart. 1993. *Why punish the children? A reappraisal of the children of incarcerated mothers in America.* San Francisco: National Council on Crime and Delinquency.

Bourdieu, P. 1977. *Outline of a theory of practice.* Translated by Richard Nice. Cambridge: Cambridge University Press.

Boyd, S. C. 1999. *Mothers and illicit drugs: Transcending the myths.* Toronto: University of Toronto Press.

———. 2000. Feminist research on mothers and illegal drugs. *Resources for Feminist Research* 28:113–32.

Brady, T. M., and O. S. Ashley, eds. 2005. *Women in substance abuse treatment: Results from the alcohol and drug services study (ADSS).* Rockville, Md.: U.S. Department of Health and Human Services, Substance Abuse and Mental Health Services Administration. http://www.oas.samhsa.gov/womenTX/ womenTX.pdf (accessed October 10, 2009).

Briere, J., R. Woo, B. McRae, J. Foltz, and R. Sitzman. 1997. Lifetime victimization history, demographics, and clinical status in female psychiatric emergency room patients. *Journal of Nervous and Mental Disease* 185:95–101.

Buffard, J. A., and F. S. Taxman. 2000. Client gender and the implementation of jail-based therapeutic community programs. *Journal of Drug Issues* 30:881–900.

Bush-Baskette, S. 2000. The war on drugs and the incarceration of mothers. *Journal of Drug Issues* 30:919–28.

Center on Addiction and Substance Abuse. 1998. *Behind bars: Substance abuse and America's prison population.* New York: Center on Addiction and Substance Abuse.

Centers for Disease Control and Prevention. 2005. Adverse childhood experiences study: Major findings. http://www.cdc.gov/nccdphp/ACE/findings.htm (accessed October 10, 2009).

Chan, M., J. Guydish, R. Prem, M. A. Jessup, A. Cervantes, and A. Bostrom. 2005. Evaluation of probation case management (PCM) for drug-involved women offenders. *Crime and Delinquency* 51:447–69.

Chesney-Lind, M. 1997. *The Female Offender: Girls, Women, and Crime.* Thousand Oaks, Calif.: Sage.

Claus, R. E., R. G. Orwin, W. Kissin, A. Krupski, K. Campbell, and K. Stark. 2007. Does gender-specific substance abuse treatment for women promote continuity of care? *Journal of Substance Abuse Treatment* 32:27–39.

Clear, T. R. 2007. *Imprisoning communities: How mass incarceration makes disadvantaged neighborhoods worse.* New York: Oxford University Press.

——— and P. Hardyman. 1990. The new intensive supervision movement. *Crime and Delinquency* 36:42–60.

Covington, S. S. 1998. The relational theory of women's psychological development: Implications for the criminal justice system. In *Female*

offenders: Critical perspectives and effective interventions, edited by R. T.
Zaplin, 113–31. Gaithersburg, Md.: Aspen.

———. 1999. *Helping women recover: A program for treating addiction.* San
Francisco: Jossey-Bass.

——— and B. Bloom. 2003. Gendered justice: Addressing female offenders. In
Gendered justice: Women in the criminal justice system, edited by B. Bloom,
1–20. Durham, N.C.: Center for Gender and Justice.

Covington, S. S., and J. L. Surrey. 1997. The relational model of women's
psychological development: Implications for substance abuse. In *Gender
and alcohol: Individual and social perspectives,* edited by R. W. Wilsnack and
S. C. Wilsnack, 335–51. New Brunswick, N.J.: Rutgers University, Center of
Alcohol Studies.

Daly, K. 1989. Gender and varieties of white-collar crime. *Criminology* 27:769–97.

———. 1992. Women's pathways to felony court: Feminist theories of
lawbreaking and problems of representation. *Southern California Review of
Law and Women's Studies* 2:11–52.

———. 1994. *Gender, crime and punishment.* New Haven, Conn.: Yale University
Press.

Ditton, P. M. 1999. *Mental health and treatment of inmates and probationers.*
Washington: Bureau of Justice Statistics.

Dvorchak, P. A., G. Grams, L. Tate, and L. A. Jason. 1995. Pregnant and postpartum
women in recovery: Barriers to treatment and the role of Oxford House in
the continuation of care. *Alcoholism Treatment Quarterly* 13:97–107.

Erez, E. 1989. Gender, rehabilitation, and probation decisions. *Criminology*
27:307–27.

Fagan, J. 1994. Women and drugs revisited: Female participation in the cocaine
economy. *Journal of Drug Issues* 24:179–225.

Farrall, S. 2003. J'accuse: Probation evaluation-research epistemologies. Part
two: This time it's personal and social factors. *Criminal Justice* 3:249–268.

——— and B. Bowling. 1999. Structuration, human development, and desistance
from crime. *British Journal of Criminology* 39:253–68.

Felitti, V. J., R. F. Anda, D. Nordenberg, D. F. Williamson, A. M. Spitz, V. Edwards,
M. P. Koss, and J. S. Marks. 1998. Relationship of childhood abuse and
household dysfunction to many of the leading causes of death in adults: The
adverse childhood experiences (ACE) study. *American Journal of Preventive
Medicine* 14:245–58.

Ferrari, J. R., L. A. Jason, R. Nelson, M. Curtin-Davis, P. Marsh, and B. Smith. 1999.
An exploratory analysis of women and men within a self-help, communal-living
recovery setting: A new beginning in a new house. *American Journal of Drug
and Alcohol Abuse* 25:305–17.

Festervan, E. 2003. *Women probationers: Supervision and success*. Lanham, Md.: American Correctional Association.

Fetterman, D. M. 1998. *Ethnography: Step by step*. Thousand Oaks, Calif.: Sage.

Fulton, B., P. Gendreau, and M. A. Paparozzi. 1995. APPA's prototypical intensive supervision program: ISP as it was meant to be. *Perspectives* 19:25–41.

Gaarder, E., N. Rodriguez, and M. S. Zatz. 2004. Criers, liars, and manipulators: Probation officers' views of girls. *Justice Quarterly* 21:547–78.

Gabel, K., and D. Johnston, eds. 1995. *Children of incarcerated parents*. New York: Lexington.

Gendreau, P., C. Goggin, and B. Fulton. 2001. Intensive supervision in probation and parole. In *Handbook of offender assessment and treatment*, edited by C. R. Hollin, 195–204. Chichester, U.K.: Wiley.

Gilligan, C. 1982. *In a different voice: Psychological theory and women's development*. Cambridge, Mass.: Harvard University Press.

Giordano, P. C., S. A. Cernkovich, and D. D. Holland, 2003. Changes in friendship relations over the life course: Implications for desistance from crime. *Criminology* 41:293–327.

Giordano, P. C., S. A. Cernkovich, and J. L. Rudolph. 2002. Gender, crime, and desistance: Toward a theory of cognitive transformation. *American Journal of Sociology* 107:990–1064.

Giordano, P. C., S. A. Cernkovich, and R. D. Schroeder. 2007. Emotions and crime over the life course: A neo-Meadian perspective on criminal continuity and change. *American Journal of Sociology* 112:1603–61.

Glaze, L. E., and T. P. Bonczar. 2007. *Probation and parole in the United States, 2006*. Washington: Bureau of Justice Statistics.

Goode, E. 1997. *Between politics and reason: The drug legalization debate*. New York: St. Martin's.

Granfield, R., and W. Cloud. 1999. *Coming clean: Overcoming addiction without treatment*. New York: New York University Press.

Greenfeld, L. A., and T. L. Snell. 1999. *Women offenders*. Washington: National Institute of Justice.

Greenfield, S. F., A. J. Brooks, S. M. Gordon, C. A. Green, F. Kropp, R. K. McHugh, M. Lincoln, D. Hien, and C. M. Miele. 2007. Substance abuse treatment entry, retention, and outcome in women: A review of the literature. *Drug and Alcohol Dependence* 86:1–21.

Griffin, M. L., and G. S Armstrong. 2003. The effect of local life circumstances on female probationers' offending. *Justice Quarterly* 20:213–39.

Gutiérrez, L., and E. Lewis. 1999. *Empowering women of color*. New York: Columbia University Press. Hannah-Moffat, K. 1999. Moral agent or actuarial subject: Risk and Canadian women's imprisonment. *Theoretical Criminology* 3:71–94.

Holtfreter, K., and M. Morash. 2003. The needs of women offenders: Implications for correctional programming. *Women and Criminal Justice* 14:137–160.

Horney, J., D. W. Osgood, and I. H. Marshall. 1995. Criminal careers in the short-term: Intra-individual variability in crime and its relation to local life circumstances. *American Sociological Review* 60:655–73.

Huddleston, C. W., D. B. Marlowe, and R. Casebolt. 2008. *Painting the current picture: A national report card on drug courts and other problem-solving court programs in the United States.* Washington: National Drug Court Institute.

Huebner, B. M. 2007. Racial and ethnic differences in the likelihood of marriage: The effect of incarceration. *Justice Quarterly* 24:156–83.

Jason, L. A., M. I. Davis, J. R. Ferrari, and P. D. Bishop. 2001. Oxford House: A review of research and implications for substance abuse recovery and community research. *Journal of Drug Education* 31:1–27.

Jessup, M., L. Edwards, T. Mason, L. Miller, and R. Katz. 2001. Therapeutic jurisprudence: Judicial and corrections panel. *Journal of Psychoactive Drugs* 33:355–67.

Johnson, H. 2004. *Drugs and crime: A study of incarcerated female offenders.* Canberra: Australian Institute of Criminology.

Kearney, M. H. 1998. Truthful self-nurturing: A grounded formal theory of women's addiction recovery. *Qualitative Health Research* 8:495–512.

Kilburn, M. R., and L. A. Karoly. 2008. *The economics of early childhood policy: What the dismal science has to say about investing in children.* Santa Monica, Calif.: RAND Corporation.

Kleinman, M. A. R., T. H. Tran, P. Fishbein, M. T. Magula, W. Allen, and G. Lacy. 2003. *Opportunities and barriers in probation reform: A case study of drug testing and sanctions.* Berkeley: California Policy Research Center.

Koons, B. A., J. D. Burrow, M. Morash, and T. S. Bynum. 1997. Expert and offender perceptions of program elements linked to successful outcomes for incarcerated women. *Crime and Delinquency* 43:512–32.

Krivo, L. J., and R. D. Peterson. 2000. The structural context of homicide: Accounting for racial differences in process. *American Sociological Review* 65:547–59.

——— , H. Rizzo, and J. Reynolds. 1998. Race, segregation, and the concentration of disadvantage: 1980–1990. *Social Problems* 45:61–80.

Ladwig, G. B., and M. D. Andersen. 1989. Substance abuse in women: Relationship between chemical dependency of women and past reports of physical and/or sexual abuse. *International Journal of the Addictions* 24:739–754.

Lahm, K. F. 2000. Equal or equitable: An exploration of educational and vocational program availability for male and female offenders. *Federal Probation* 64:39–46.

Langan, N., and B. Pelissier. 2001. Gender differences among prisoners in drug treatment. *Journal of Substance Abuse Treatment* 13:291–301.

Laub, J. H., D. S. Nagin, and R. J. Sampson. 1998. Trajectories of change in criminal offending: Good marriages and the desistance process. *American Sociological Review* 63:225–38.

Laub, J. H., and R. J. Sampson. 2001. Understanding desistance from crime. In *Crime and justice: A review of research*, edited by M. Tonry, 1–69. Chicago: University of Chicago Press.

Leshner, A. I. 1997. Addiction is a brain disease, and it matters. *Science* 278:45–47.

Link, P., and J. Phelan. 2001. Conceptualizing stigma. *Annual Review of Sociology* 27:363–85.

Lipsey, M. W., N. A. Landenberger, and S. J. Wilson. 2007. *Effects of cognitive-behavioral programs for criminal offenders*. Nashville, Tenn.: Vanderbilt Institute for Public Policy Studies.

Little Hoover Commission. 2004. *Breaking the barriers for women on parole.* Sacramento, Calif.: Little Hoover Commission. http://www.lhc.ca.gov/studies/177/report177.html, accessed June 15, 2009.

Logan, T. K., R. Walker, J. Cole, and C. Leukefel. 2002. Victimization and substance abuse among women: Contributing factors, interventions, and implications. *Review of General Psychiatry* 6:325–97.

Longshore, D., S. Turner, and T. Fain. 2005. Effects of case management on parolee misconduct: The Bay Area services network. *Criminal Justice and Behavior* 32:205–22.

Maher, L. 2000. *Sexed work: Gender, race, and resistance in a Brooklyn drug market.* New York: Oxford University Press.

Maruna, S. 2000. *Making good: How ex-convicts reform and rebuild their lives.* Washington: American Psychological Association.

Mauer, M., and M. Chesney-Lind, eds. 2002. *Invisible punishment: The collateral consequences of mass imprisonment.* Washington: Sentencing Project.

McKay, J. R., T. R. Franklin, N. Patapis, and K. G. Lynch. 2006. Conceptual, methodological, and analytical issues in the study of relapse. *Clinical Psychology Review* 26:109–27.

McMahon, M., ed. 2000. *Assessment to assistance: Programs for women in community corrections.* Lexington, Ky.: American Probation and Parole Association.

Miller, E. M. 1986. *Street woman.* Philadelphia: Temple University Press.

Monture-Angus, P. 2000. Aboriginal women and correctional practice: Reflections on the task force on federally sentenced women. In *An ideal prison? Critical essays on women's imprisonment in Canada*, edited by K. Hannah-Moffat and M. Shaw, 52–60. Halifax, Nova Scotia: Fernwood.

Moore, L. D., and A. Elkavich. 2008. Who's using and who's doing time. *American Journal of Public Health* 98:782–86.

Morash, M. 2006. *Understanding gender, crime, and justice*. Thousand Oaks, Calif.: Sage.

———, T. S. Bynum, and B. Koons. 1996. *Findings from the national study of innovative and promising programs for women offenders*. East Lansing: Michigan State University.

Morash, M., and A. L. Robinson. 2002. Correctional administrators' perspectives on gender arrangements and family-related programming for women offenders. *Marriage and Family Review* 32:83–109.

Mullany, J. M. 2002. Special conditions for female probationers: Disparity or discrimination. *Justice Professional* 15:169–80.

Murphy, S., and P. Sales. 2001. Pregnant drug users: Scapegoats of Reagan/Bush and Clinton-era economics. *Social Justice* 28:72–95.

National Institute of Justice. 2006. *Drug courts: The second decade*. Washington: U.S. Department of Justice, National Institute of Justice. http://www.ncjrs .gov/pdffiles1/nij/211081.pdf, accessed October 11, 2009.

Needle, R. H., and A. Mills. 1994. *Drug procurement practices of the out-of-treatment chronic drug abuser*. Rockville, Md.: U.S. Department of Health and Human Services, National Institute on Drug Abuse.

Nurco, D. N., T. E. Hanlon, T. W. Kinlock, and K. R. Duszynski. 1988. Differential criminal patterns of narcotic addicts over an addiction career. *Criminology* 26:407–23

O'Brien, P. 2001. "Just like baking a cake": Women describe the necessary ingredients for successful reentry after incarceration. *Families in Society* 82:287–95.

———. 2006. Maximizing success for drug-affected women after release from prison: Examining access to and use of social services during reentry. *Women and Criminal Justice* 17:95–113.

——— and N. J. Harm. 2002. Women's recidivism and reintegration: Two sides of the same coin. In *Women at the margins: Neglect, punishment, and resistance*, edited by J. Figueira-McDonough and R. C. Sarri, 295–318. New York: Haworth.

O'Brien, P., and D. S. Young. 2006. Challenges for formerly incarcerated women: A holistic approach to assessment families in society. *Journal of Contemporary Social Services* 87:359–66.

Owen, B., and B. Bloom. 1995. Profiling women prisoners: Findings from national surveys and a California sample. *Prison Journal* 75:165–85.

Paparozzi, M. A., and P. Gendreau. 2005. An intensive supervision program that worked: Service delivery, professional orientation, and organizational supportiveness. *Prison Journal* 85:445–66.

Parsons, M. L., C. Warner-Robbins, and M. Parsons. 2002. Factors that support women's successful transition to the community following jail/prison. *Health Care for Women International* 23:6–18.

Peele, S. 1985. *The meaning of addiction: Compulsive experience and its interpretation.* Lexington, Mass.: Lexington.

Peters, R. H., A. L. Strozier, M. R. Murrin, and W. D. Kearns. 1997. Treatment of substance-abusing jail inmates: Examination of gender differences. *Journal of Substance Abuse Treatment* 14:339–49.

Petersilia, J., and S. Turner. 1993. Intensive probation and parole. *Crime and Justice* 17:281–335.

Piliavin, I., R. Gartner, and C. Thornton. 1986. Crime, deterrence, and rational choice. *American Sociological Review* 51:101–19.

Prendergast, M. L., J. Wellisch, and G. Falkin. 1995. Assessment of and services for substance abusing women offenders in community and correctional settings. *Prison Journal* 75:240–56.

Proctor, B. D., and J. Dalaker. 2003. *Poverty in the United States: 2002.* Washington: U.S. Census Bureau.

Reed, B. G., and M. E. Leavitt. 1998. "Modified wrap around and women offenders: A community corrections continuum." Paper presented at the International Community Corrections Annual Conference, Arlington, Va.

Research Triangle International and Urban Institute. 2004. *National portrait of SVORI: Serious and violent offender reentry initiative.* Research Triangle Park, N.C.: Research Triangle International.

Richie, B. E. 1996. *Compelled to crime: The gender entrapment of battered black women.* New York: Routledge.

———. 2001. Challenges incarcerated women face as they return to their communities: Findings from life history interviews. *Crime and Delinquency* 47:368–89.

Rumgay, J. 2004. Living with paradox: Community supervision of women offenders. In *Women who offend,* edited by G. McIvor, 99–125. Philadelphia: Jessica Kingsley.

Ruspini, E. 2002. *Introduction to longitudinal research.* London: Routledge.

Sabol, W. J., H. Couture, and P. M. Harrison. 2007. *Prisoners in 2006.* Washington: U.S. Department of Justice.

Sampson, R. J., and J. H. Laub. 1993. *Crime in the making: Pathways and turning points through life.* Cambridge, Mass.: Harvard University Press.

Schaffner, L. 2006. *Girls in trouble with the law.* New Brunswick, N.J.: Rutgers University Press.

Schram, P. J., B. A. Koons-Witt, F. P. Williams, and M. D. McShane. 2006. Supervision strategies and approaches for female parolees: Examining the link between unmet needs and parolee outcome. *Crime and Delinquency* 52:450–71.

Schroeder, R. D., P. C. Giordano, and S. A. Cernkovich. 2007. Drug use and desistance processes. *Criminology* 45:191–222.

Seng, M., and A. J. Lurigio. 2005. Probation officers' views on supervising women probationers. *Women and Criminal Justice* 16:65–86.

Seymour, C. 1998. Children with parents in prison: Child welfare policy, program, and practice issues. *Child Welfare* 77:469–93.

Shaw, M. 1996. Is there a feminist future for women's prisons? In *Prisons 2000: An international perspective on the current state and future of imprisonment*, edited by R. Matthews and P. Francis, 179–200. London: Macmillan.

Sherman, F. 2003. *Girls in the juvenile justice system: Perspectives on services and conditions of confinement*. Boston: Girls' Justice Initiative.

Shover, N. 1996. *Great pretenders: Pursuits and careers of persistent thieves*. Boulder, Colo.: Westview.

———— and C. Y. Thompson. 1992. Age, differential expectations, and crime desistance. *Criminology* 30:89–104.

Siefert, K., and S. Pimlott. 2001. Improving pregnancy outcome during imprisonment: A model residential care program. *Social Work* 46:125–34.

Simpson, S. S., J. L. Yahner, and L. Dugan. 2009. Understanding women's pathways to jail: Analyzing the lives of incarcerated women. *Australian and New Zealand Journal of Criminology* 41:84–108.

Skeem, J. L., J. Eno Louden, S. Manchak, S. Vidal, and E. Haddad. 2009. Social networks and social control of probationers with co-occurring mental and substance abuse problems. *Law and Human Behavior* 33:122–35.

Skeem, J. L., J. Eno Louden, D. Polaschek, and J. Camp. 2007. Assessing relationship quality in mandated community treatment: Blending care with control. *Psychological Assessment* 19:397–410.

Smart, C., and B. Smart. 1978. Women and social control: An introduction. In *Women, sexuality and social control*, edited by C. Smart and B. Smart, 1–7. London: Routledge and Kegan Paul.

Steadman, H. J., F. C. Osher, P. C. Robbins, B. Case, and S. Samuels. 2009. Prevalence of serious mental illness among jail inmates. *Psychiatric Services* 60:761–65.

Substance Abuse and Mental Health Services Administration. 2002. *Results from the 2001 national household survey on drug abuse*. Vol. 1, *Summary of National Findings*. Rockville, Md.: U.S. Department of Health and Human Services, Substance Abuse and Mental Health Services Administration.

http://www.oas.samhsa.gov/nhsda/2k1nhsda/PDF/cover.pdf, accessed October 11, 2009.

Uggen, C., and C. Kruttschnitt. 1998. Crime in the breaking: Gender differences in desistance. *Law and Society Review* 32:339–66.

Uggen, C., and M. Thompson. 2003. The socioeconomic determinants of ill-gotten gains: Within-person changes in drug use and illegal earnings. *American Journal of Sociology* 109:146–85.

U.S. Department of Justice. 2008. *Prisoners in 2007*. Washington: U.S. Department of Justice.

Veysey, B. M., R. Andersen, L. Lewis, M. Mueller, and V. M. K. Stenius. 2005. Integration of alcohol and other drug, trauma and mental health services: An experiment in rural services integration in Franklin County, MA. *Alcoholism Treatment Quarterly* 22:19–39.

Veysey, B. M., J. Heckman, R. Mazelis, L. Markoff, and L. Russell. 2007. *It's my time to live: Journeys to healing and recovery*. Washington: U.S. Department of Health and Human Services, Substance Abuse and Mental Health Services Administration.

Vogt, I. 1998. Gender and drug treatment systems. In *Drug treatment systems in an international perspective: Drugs, demons, and delinquents*, edited by H. Klingemann and G. Hunt, 281–97. Thousand Oaks, Calif.: Sage.

Walitzer, K. S., and R. L. Dearing. 2006. Gender differences in alcohol and substance use relapse. *Clinical Psychology Review* 26:128–48.

Warr, M. 1998. Life course transitions and desistance from crime. *Criminology* 36:183–216.

Wellisch, J., M. L. Prendergast, and M. D. Anglin. 1994. *Drug-abusing women offenders: Results of a national survey*. Washington: U.S. Department of Justice.

Wu, L. T., and C. Ringwalt. 2005. Use of substance abuse services by young uninsured American adults. *Psychiatric Services* 56:946–53.

Young, A. M., C. Boyd, and H. Hubbell. 2000. Prostitution, drug use, and coping with psychological distress. *Journal of Drug Issues* 30:789–800.

Zaplin, R. T. 1998. Female offenders: A systems perspective. In *Female offenders: Critical perspectives and effective interventions*, edited by R. Zaplin, 65–80. Gaithersburg, Md.: Aspen.